HANDBOOK OF ORGANIC FARMING AND BIO-FERTILIZERS

Handbook of Organic Farming and Bio-Fertilizers

M.K. Gupta

ABD PUBLISHERS
Jaipur ■ New Delhi

ABD PUBLISHERS

Regd. Off. "Bony Residency", Gate No. 2
Opp. Tilak Public School, Vishweswariya Nagar,
Gopalpura Road, Jaipur - 302018, India
Ph: 0141 - 2761280, Telefax: 2761381
Email: abdpublishersjpr@gmail.com

Delhi Office: 102, 1st Floor, Satyam House,
4327/3, Ansari Road, Darya Ganj,
New Delhi - 110002, India
Ph: 011-45652440

visit us: www.oxfordbookcompany.com

Distributor By
KEYA INTERNATIONAL PRESS LLP
E-mail: keyainternationalpressllp@gmail.com

Published in India, 2024

ISBN: 9788183761109

Typeset by Shivangi Computer, Jaipur

Printed and bound in India by Thomson Press Ltd.,
New Delhi

Preface

Food security is the right of each and every one irrespective of economic status. Looking to the increasing population it is necessary to increase the food production to meet out the increased demand of food. Basically there are two ways of increasing food production - by increasing land under farming and by increasing the productivity of the soil. While first option is practically not possible since ploughable land is decreasing as more and more agricultural land is being utilised to meet increasing urbanisation; the scientists have given more emphasis on devising means to increase the productivity of soil.

Organic farming is a system of agriculture that seeks to maintain and improve productivity of land as for as possible by encouraging and enhancing natural biological processes in the soil. Discarding the use of expensive resources and chemicals, it lays emphasis on the need to understand natural process and non-destructive management. While modern agriculture based on use of chemical fertilizers, pesticides, etc., favour the growth of one facet and eliminates or reduces the others resulting in ecological imbalance between components of ecosystem, organic farming favours the natural activities and thus ecosystem is maintained making it sustainable allowing the coexistence of plants, animals, insects, microbes, etc.

Bio-fertilizers are the products containing living cells of different types of microorganism which have an ability to mobilise nutritionally important elements from non-usable to usable form through biological process. Bio-fertilizers are environment friendly, low cost, non bulky agricultural input which significantly improves soil fertility and plant nutrition. More and more people in the world are using and favouring organic farming and use of bio-fertilizers. As such the field is attracting keen interest.

- M.K. Gupta

Contents

Chapter 1

Concept of Organic Farming in IPNS

S.C. Bhandari
Dept. of Agri. Chem. & Soil Science, RCA, Udaipur

Introduction

Food security is the right and it should be available to each and every body irrespective of economic status. Looking to the increasing population, it is necessary to increase the food production at the same pace. Food security helps in fighting against malnutrition and hunger because import of grain is costly and unreliable. Basically there are two ways of increasing foodgrain—by increasing land under plough which is practically not possible rather it is decreasing as more and more agricultural land is going under urbanisation and second and only alternative is to increase the productivity of soil.

Although, green revolution resulted in increased food production many fold but also resulted in increased demand for fertilizers, agricultural chemicals, energy and are causing pollution of soil, water and air. As such there is question mark in sustainability of modern agriculture which brought the country to self sufficiency in foodgrain.

Organic farming is a system of agriculture that seeks to maintain and improve productivity of land as far as possible by encouraging and enhancing natural biological processes. Rejecting the use of resources extravagant and energy demanding chemicals, it lays stress on the need to understand natural process and non-destructive management. Organic farming as a matter of fact is an agricultural philosophy and a farm management system. It is a farming of permanency and aimed at promoting plant, animal and human health (Somani *et al.*, 1992).

Available Resources

Land, water and solar energy are principal natural resources for sustaining life on earth. Table 1 shows the available resources (1993-94) with 142.1 mha as net area sown (46.6%) and 68.42 mha under forest. Net irrigated area is 57.45 mha and crop intensity is only 131.19 per cent (Annon. 1997).

Table 1

Available Resources of India (1993-94) (mha)

1.	Geographical area	328.73
2.	Forest	68.42
3.	Net available for cultivation	41.00
4.	Net area sown	142.1
5.	Total cropped area	186.42
6.	Area sown more than once	44.32
7.	Cropping intensity	131.19%
8.	Net irrigated area	57.45
9.	Gross irrigated area	68.37

Source: *Fertilizer Statistics* (1989-90).

Constraints of Modern Agriculture

Modern agriculture based on extensive cultivation, and use of chemical fertilizers, high yielding varieties responsive to nutrients, use of plant protection chemicals have posed that problems resulting in risk of pollution to natural resources and reached to a stage of stagnation in yield. The degree of land degradation is evident from the data presented in Table 2.

Table 2
Extent of Land Degradation in India (mha)

1.	Wind and water erosion	144.4
2.	Degraded through specific problem	
	(a) Waterlogged	8.5
	(b) Alkalinity	3.6
	(c) Salinity	5.5
	(d) Ravines and Gullies	3.9
	(e) Shifting cultivation	4.9
	(f) Ravines and Torrents	2.7
3.	Total problem area	173.5
4.	Loss of nutrients annually	5.4 - 8.4 mt
5.	Loss of production due to development of ravines	3 mt
6.	Encroachment to arable land by ravines annually	8 mha
7.	Flood prone area	40 mha
8.	Drought prone area	260 mha

Source: *Fertilizer Statistics* (1989-90).

Too much tillage operation, use of heavy machines, decreasing recycling of crop residues have resulted in deterioration of soil physical properties like apparent density, texture, structure etc. Intensive cropping, loss of nutrients through volatilisation, leaching and denitrification, excess removal and limited supplementation have resulted in wide spread decrease in soil fertility status. It has also resulted in increased deficiency of micronutrients and imbalance of nutrients (Dev, 1996), although fertilizer consumption increased from 65600 tonnes in 1951-52 to 13876100 tonnes in 1995-96 (Annon., 1997). Compared to many countries, fertilizer application in India is very low.

Growth and yield of crop plants depend on the health of soil, quality of water and atmospheric pollution. Rapid and unorganised growth of industries, increasing number of vehicles, mismanagement of natural resource - soil through discriminate use of fertilizer and pesticides have resulted in pollution of resources like soil, underground water and surface water and air and situation has reached to a alarming level in some cases like river and ponds water, air especially of cities and towns. Use of synthetic pesticides have resulted in pollution of resources as well as it has been detected in food articles and human body resulting in many complexes (Vyas *et al.*, 1996).

Organic Farming

Modern agriculture based on use of chemical fertilizers, pesticides, irrigation favours the growth of one facet and eliminates or reduces the others resulting in ecological imbalance between components of eco-systems. Whereas, organic farming favours the natural activities and thus ecosystem is maintained and that is why it is sustainable. It allows the coexistence of plants—animals—insects—microbes. Concept of organic farming gives emphasis on aspects like:

Land use planning

Proper land use planning allow long-term profitable use of land resources without deterioration and highest return. The use of land for cultivation, grazing, forest, recreation, roads, city etc. should be according to its limitation with best land under cultivation. Proper use would also increase the efficiency of other inputs like water, nutrients, varieties etc. on account of reduced losses etc.

Reduced tillage and conservation of resources

Tillage of soil is essential for good germination and establishment of seedlings but excess results in loss or soil, water, nutrients, energy etc. It also increases the cost of production. Maintenance of soil organic carbon is possible by minimum tillage practice.

Integrated nutrient supply

Recycling of organic wastes of crops, fruits and vegetables, forests, aquatic etc. reduces the demand of plant nutrients through fertilizers as they have a potential of about 13 mt of nutrients (Vimal and Talashilkar, 1983). The efficiency of these sources can be improved by the supplementing with chemicals and biological agents (Mishra *et al.,* 1989). The efficiency of compost can also be improved by mediating it with earthworms. Use of these resources improve the physical properties as well biological properties of soils. Bio-fertilizers are another eco-friendly component of IPN and results in reduced demand of fertilizer (Somani *et al.*, 1990).

Integrated pest management

Continuous discriminate use of chemicals result in lowering down of efficiency and increased resistance to chemicals in addition to environmental pollution. The recent need for sustainable agriculture demands for exploitation of natural predators, parasites, plant extracts, cultural practices, resistant varieties etc. coupled with chemicals wherever necessary so as to reduce the use of chemicals (Pathak, 1992).

Water resources

Water is scarce input and its judicious use is essential. Discriminate use results in salt problems, leaching losses, soil erosion, water logging etc. Judicious use through adoption of mulching, compaction, low water requiring crops, improved water application methods like sprinkler, drip etc. help in improving the use efficiency. Water harvesting of rain water *in situ* and through watershed management help in reducing load over other irrigation resources (Mahnot and Singh, 1992).

Integrated farming

Principally integrated or mixed farming involves crops, livestock, poultry piggery, sericulture, fisheries, apiculture, forestry, apiculture, mushroom etc. so as to use non-renewable resources, time, human power and renewable resources in whole system involving soil-plant-animal. It utilises the waste/byproduct of one by another in total or partial so as to increase the productivity of farm per unit of land per unite time and generating income.

Energy

Input of energy in one or other form is essential for any operation. Emphasis should be given towards maximum use of renewable resources like air, solar, bio-energy etc. It is possible only when plants having higher photosynthetic efficiency are used to harvest maximum solar energy along with use of other system of harvesting renewable sources and also recycle of so trapped energy.

Conclusion

Sustainable agriculture with minimum dependence inputs like fertilizer, pesticides etc. is possible by adopting technologies which enhances natural reactions without disturbing the ecological balance through organic farming wherein recycling of organic carbon maintenance of soil plant - animal - microbes balance and limited and judicious use of natural resources are allowed.

References

Annon. 1997. In: *Agricultural Statistics at a Glance*, Directorate of Economics & Statistics, Ministry of Agriculture, New Delhi.

Dev. G. 1996. *Balanced Fertilizer Use for Increasing Foodgrains Production in Western States*. PPIC, Gurgaon, (Haryana).

Mahnot, S. C. and Singh, A.K. 1992. In: *Proc. Nat. Seminar Natural Farming* (Ed. L.L. Somani, K.L. Totawat and B.L. Baser) Raj College of Agriculture, Udaipur.

Mishra, M.M.; Kukreja, K.; Kappor, K.K. and Bangar, K.C. 1989. In : *Soil Micro-organisms and Crop Growth* (ed. L.L. Somani and S.C. Bhandari), Divyajyoti Prakashan, Jodhpur.

Pathak, V.N. 1992. In: *Proc. Nat. Seminar Natural Farming* (Ed. L.L. Somani, K.L. Totawat and B.L. Baser), Raj College of Agriculture, Udaipur.

Somani, L.L.; Bhandari, S.C.; Saxena, S.N. and Vyas, K.K. 1990. *Bio-fertilizers*. Scientific Publishers, Jodhpur.

Somani, L.L.; Totawat, K.L. and Baser, B.L. 1992. *Proc. Nat Sem. Natural Farming*, Raj. College of Agriculture, Udaipur.

Vimal, O.P. and Talashilkar, S. 1983. *J. Sci. Ind. Res*. 42 : 115.

Vyas, K.K.; Bhandari, S.C. and Singh, S.D. 1996. *Mrida Vigyan*, Rajasthan Hindi Granth Academy, Jaipur.

Chapter 2

Bio-Fertilizers: A Supplemental Source of Plant Nutrients in IPNS

L.L. Somani
Dept. of Agri. Chem. & Soil Science, RCA, Udaipur

Introduction

With almost twice the quantity of plant nutrients being removed from soil than what is added through fertilizers, the growing nutrient imbalance poses a major threat to sustain soil health and crop productivity. Commercial fertilizers have had a substantial effect on world's food production. In fact, these have played a key role in ushering in the Green Revolution. While the use of chemical fertilizers is the quickest and surest way of boosting crop production, their cost and others constraints frequently deter farmers from using them in recommended quantities and in balanced proportions. The modern agricultural practices being too intensive often result in imbalance in the soil reserves which, in turn, not only effect microbial ecology, but also the fertilizer use efficiency. There has been decline in crop yields even under continuous use of chemical fertilizers.

The use of chemical fertilizers not only depletes the non-renewable natural reserves of fossil fuel but also adds to the cost of production. Moreover, because of their low use efficiency, high depends on chemical fertilizers besides polluting underground water also pollutes the atmosphere through volatilisation and de-nitrification destroying protective ozone layer. Economic and environmental considerations are thus compelling us to find sustainable alternatives. Though, we cannot avoid the use of chemical fertilizers altogether, our production targets must be linked to with a desire for sustainability by exploiting potential alternative sources of plant nutrients.

IPNS and Bio-Fertilizers

In coming decades, a major issue in designing sustainable agricultural system will be the management of soil organic matter and the rational use of biological and organic inputs such as bio-fertilizers, animal manure, crop residues, green manures, sewage sludge and food industry wastes. Since neither bio-fertilizers nor organic sources can meet the total nutrient needs of modern agriculture, integrated use of nutrients from fertilizers, bio-fertilizers and organic sources seems to be a need of the time.

An integrated approach is one in which more than one management factors are combined and interacted for better utilisation of resources and ultimately higher yields. The appropriate combination of chemical fertilizers, bio-fertilizers, organic manures etc. varies according to the system of land use and ecological, social and economic conditions. The basic concept underlying the IPNS is the maintenance and possible improvement of soil fertility for sustained crop productivity on long-term basis besides reducing fertilizer input cost. The different components of IPNS possess great diversity in terms of chemical and physical properties and nutrient release patterns. IPNS puts the local resources to the best and maximum use which fits well into the philosophy of low cost technology needed for the small and marginal farmers.

Bio-fertilizers

Bio-fertilizers are the products containing living cells of different types of micro-organisms which have an ability to mobilise nutritionally important element from non-usable to usable form through biological process. Some soil micro-organisms play an important role in improving soil fertility and crop productivity due to their capability to fix atmospheric nitrogen, solubilise insoluble phosphate and decompose farm wastes resulting in the release of plant nutrients. The extent of benefit from these micro-organisms depends upon their number and efficiency, which, however, is governed by a large number of soil and environmental factors. When the number and activity of specific micro-organisms is sub-optimal, artificially multiplied culture of that micro-organisms called 'bio-fertilizers' is used to hasten biological activity to improve the availability of plant nutrient. Seeds, seedlings or soils are treated with these bio-fertilizers to facilitate increase their numbers in the soil or rhizosphere. Bio-fertilizers are apparently environment friendly, low cost, non-bulky agricultural input which could play a significant role in plant nutrition as supplementary and complementary factor to mineral nutrition.

The term Bio-fertilizers has been coined to embody all such micro-organisms which add, conserve and mobilise the plant nutrients in the soil. Such micro-organisms have somehow come to be called as "bio-fertilizers," a term which is a misnomer, compared to commercial fertilizers manufactured on a large scale by factories. In other words, bio-fertilizers are based on renewable energy sources and are eco-friendly compared to commercial fertilizers.

Bio-fertilizers play a very significant role in improving soil fertility by fixing atmospheric nitrogen, both, in association with plant roots and without it, solubilise soil phosphates and produce plant; growth substances in the soil.

Classification

Depending upon the nutrient provided, Verma and Bhattacharyya (1994) have broadly classified bio-fertilizers as follows:

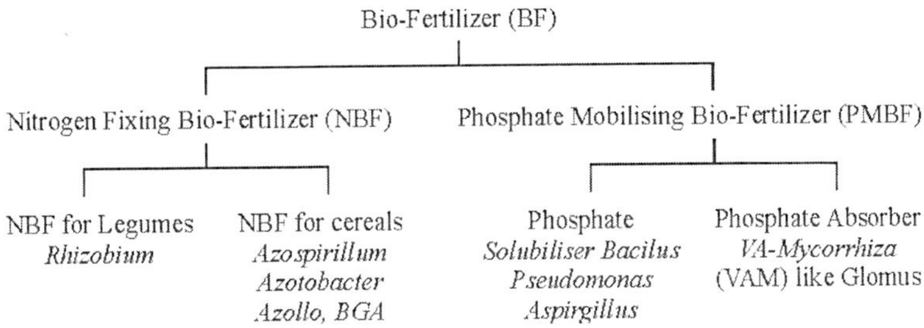

Characteristics of various bio-fertilizers listed above follows:

Rhizobium

The role of legumes in enriching the fertility of soil by contributing nitrogen through symbiotic nitrogen fixation by *Rhizobium* is well established.

Nodulation

The free living rhizobia infects the host legume through infection thread or at the point of emergence of lateral roots and are transferred into bacteroids which are the site of nitrogen fixation (Somani and Bhandari, 1990). The root cap cells secrete large amounts of polysaccharides forming mucigel in which rhizobia are found enmeshed in large number. Curling and branching of root hair is the first visible plant response to rhizobia (Nutman, 1959). Localised auxin production by *Rhizobium* at the root hair surface softens the cell wall to facilitate infection thread for transference of the bacterial cells into root cortex. The thread grows with the growth rate of the hair itself (Dart, 1977). Rhizobia get trapped within the fold of growing, deformed hair, inducing wall synthesis to enclose the rhizobia.

Cross Inoculation Groups

Legumes can be divided into groups based on specificity for *Rhizobium* spp (Fred *et al.*, 1932). For example lupinus do not nodulate when inoculated with cultures from pea, and that *Phaseolus* and *Pisum* did not nodulate with isolates from *lupinus* or *Robinia i.e.* such cross infection is not possible. These observations gave birth to the concept of cross inoculation group–that separate *Rhizobium* species only nodulate specific related legumes. Fahraeus and Ljunggren (1968) postulated that Rhizobium strains capable of infecting a legume release a specific polysaccharide that induces pectolytic activity by the root which account for the cross inoculation specificities. This activity, by loosening the root hair wall structure, would facilitate infection thread initiation.

Mechanism of N-fixation

The nodulate is simply a protective structure and that bacteroids are the seats of N-fixation. Reduction of N_2 to NH_3 is mediated through enzyme nitrogenase which is made up of two components—one with Fe + Mo and the second without Mo (Quispel, 1974). N-fixation is an anaerobic process. The oxygen supply to bacteroid is excluded due to presence of leghaemoglobin around it. The leghamoglobin provides a membraneous envelope around bactyeroids. This pigment limits oxygen supply and helps in providing low oxygen conditions near the bacteroids and thus protects the oxygen sensitive nitrogenase from damage. Enough oxygen, however, is made available at the site for generation of ATP. The quantum of N-fixed is closely related to the amount of leghaemoglobin and the extent of bacteroid tissues is nodules (Bergersen and Briggs, 1958).

A source of ATP and nitrogenase are essential for nitrogenase catalysed reaction. Products of photosynthesis are translocated from leaves to nodules providing thereby the needed ATP and reluctant for N-fixation. The iron of haemoglobin is believed to be involved in the binding of nitrogenase while molybdenum is responsible for the decrease in the strength of nitrogen bonds (N=N) to an optimum extent to facilitate reduction. The enzyme nitrogenase couples ATP hydrolysis to ADP with electron transfer from a reduced electron doner (Ferredoxin of flavodoxin) to reduce N_2 to NH_3. The first stable intermediate in N-fixation is ammonia.

Factors Affecting Nodulation and N-fixation

There is a marked effect of genetic characters of the host plant on the results of symbiosis, plants sensitive to nodulaton have a high C/N ratio (Hubbel and Elkan, 1967). Host plant is the dominant factor in assessing effective and ineffective strains of rhizobia (Burton *et al.,* 1954). The poor N-fixing ability of some otherwise effective strains of rhizobia, under field conditions has been attributed to antagonistic microflora (Burton, 1964). There is a direct relationship between light intensity, nodulation and N-fixation (Gibson, 1977) by affecting photosynthesis and supply of carbohydrates to Rhizobium. Nodule development is retarded by high light intensities because the amount of nitrogen available for the nodule is reduced due to large increase in the level of carbohydrates in the plant tissues. Rhizobia die rapidly under drying conditions (Tilak, 1991). Biologically formed toxins may influence the establishment of rhizobia on roots (Chatel and Parker, 1972). Predation by high population of indigenous protozoa (which feed upon *Rhizobium*) is an important factor in reducing the population of *Rhizobium* (Danso *et al.,* 1975). Nodulation is much adversely affected by soil acidity than the development of roots (Mulder *et al.,* 1966). Acid soil frequently contain levels of Al, Mn, or Fe that are injurious to nodulation or growth of rhizobia. Salinity induced delay in nodulation may result in reduced yields (Bhardwaj, 1975). Seed applied fungicides are not specific for plant pathogens or even fungi, and may kill rhizobia and render useless the added inoculant (Chendrayan and Prasad, 1976).

High doses of nitrogenous fertilizer decreased the N-fixation, whereas lower dose increased the symbiosis and growth of the legume (Bazyrina *et al.,* 1949). Calcium is highly essential to growth of rhizobia. Cobalt is an important growth factor for rhizobia. Molybdenum plays an important role in the transfer of electrons. Elements like iron, copper and cobalt have been implicated in leghaemoglobin synthesis (Burris, 1966).

Crop Response to Rhizobium

Inoculation of legumes with effective strains of *Rhizobium* has been found to increase legume yields by 6-65 per cent over uninoculated controls (Subba Rao and Tilak, 1984). The quantum of nitrogen fixed by legume - rhizobium symbiosis has been reported to vary from 13 to 360 kg N/ha/season depending upon legume species, host *Rhizobium* genotype, agroclimatic conditions and their interaction (Danso *et al.,* 1972; Keyse and Li, 1992; Gupta and Pandher, 1996).

Azotobacter

The Organism

Azotobacter is one of the most important non-symbiotic N-fixing micro-organism and is considered to be very important for fixation of nitrogen in non-leguminous plants. Based on morphological and physiological features, the genus *Azotobacter* has been classified in three species *A. Chroococcum, A. Beijerinckii* and *A. Vinelandii.* The first two species are deemed to be the most commonly occurring species in India. *Azotobacter chroococcum* appeared in acid soils while *A. Beijerinckii* in neutral and alkali soils.

Factors Affecting Azotobacter Growth

Azotobacter are mesophilic bacteria. The optimum temperature for its growth is 25-35^{0}C (Blinkov, 1955). *Azotobacter* cells require high humidity, the growth commencement require soil humidity of at least 20 per cent of saturation (Mishustin, 1954). *Azotobacter* is resistant to high salt concentration (Kvasnikov, 1956). Optimum pH for *Azotobacter* growth was shown to lie near or slightly above neutrality (Blinkov, 1955). The minimum and maximum pH where *Azotobacter* can grow have been reported to 4.5 and 10 (Yamagata and Itano, 1923; Roizin and Ezrukh, 1958). *Azotobacter* cells are killed with dressing of seeds with formalin (Ezubchik 1939). Deep tillage has been found to enhance *Azotobacter* (Geller, 1958). Free nitrogen and NH_4-N are antagonist (Fedorov, 1952). Deficiency of Mo may led to failure of *Azotobacter* growth (Bostels, 1939).

Crop Response to Azotobacter

Azotobacter has been found to increase crop yields by 0-30 per cent (Venkataraman and Tilak, 1990). Morris *et al.* (1978) did not find any beneficial effect of *Azotobacter* inoculation on corn, cotton, oat and wheat. The attributed local conditions of soil fertility and environment as main factors for non-beneficial effect of *Azotobacter* strains. Genetic variability for response to Azotobacter has been noted in different wheat cultivars (Bishnoi *et al.,* 1995). The use of themotolerant strains of *Azotobacter* for cotton has been recommended by Kumar *et al.,* (1995) who reported that *Azotobacter* inoculation caused 18 per cent increase in N content of shoots of cotton crop. Gupta and Pandher (1996) reported yield increase of 0-47 for a number of corps. The nitrogen fixation by *Azotobacter* is about 20-40 kg N/ha.

Azospirillum

The Organism

Beyerinck (1925) first described *Spirillum Lipoferum* as a possible nitrogen fixer. Dobereiner and Day (1976) found a significant correlation between the numbers of these organisms and the nitrogenase activity of small root pieces. Since that time spirilla have been found to be associated with the roots and rhizosphere of many other members of the Gramineae (Lehri and Tiwari, 1989). The nomenclature of this organism was revised and designated as

Azospirillum (Terrand *et al.,* 1978). There are four major species of *Azospirillum viz. A. Lipoferum, A. Brasilense, A. Amazonense* and *A. Seropedicae*. Of the four species, first two species are commonly found. *A. Lipoferum* is commonly found in the roots of C_4 plants, while *A. Brasilense* is found in C_3 plants in tropical and subtropical regions (Patriquin, 1990). Knowledge of the specificity of association between *Azospirillum* and various grasses and cereals may have significant implications in establishing N-fixing associations with selected strains of bacteria (Baldani and Dobereiner, 1980).

Crop Response to Azospirillum

The *Azospirillum* inoculation has been found beneficial in a variety of crops. The crop response varies greatly with types of crop and variety, location, season, soil fertility level, native microbial interaction etc. Crop response to *Azospirillum* is attributed to its ability to fix atmospheric nitrogen and to produce phytohormones (Summer, 1990). On an average, an increase of about 200-300 kg/ha in crop yields and an economy of 20-30 kg N/ha equivalent is possible by *Azospirillum* inoculation (Venkataraman and Tilak, 1990). Inoculation of sorghum with *A. Lipoferum* produced 38 per cent increase in dry matter over uninoculated control (Wani *et al.,* 1980). Subba Rao *et al.,* (1983) reported yield increases of 9-30 per cent as a consequence of *Azospirillum* inoculation of finger millet.

Azolla

The Organism

Azolla is a genus of elegant water ferns that are widely distributed in fresh water systems. This fern is commonly found in ponds, ditches, canals, rice fields. All species of this fern harbour the N_2-fixing alga *Anabaena azollae* in their leaf cavities as symbiont. Azolla provide protected environment and nutrients to the *Anabaena* in exchange for the fixed N (Ashton and Walmsley, 1976). *Azolla - Anabaena azollae* system is very attractive because the symbiont is efficient in N_2-fixation and the fern grows on swampy lands that also favour growth of the rice. Rice growing areas in south-east Asia and other third world countries have recently been evincing increased interest in the use of N_2 fixing water fern *Azolla* either as an alternate nitrogen source or as a supplement to commercial nitrogen fertilizers (Watanabe, 1982). Tran and Dao (1973) provided good evidence that *Azolla* incorporation into the soil as a green manure crop is one of the most effective ways of providing N to rice. The utilisation of *Azolla* as a fuel crop with wetland rice is gaining increasing importance (Kannaiyan, 1992). The important factor in using *Azolla* as bio-fertilizer is its fast growth rate with a doubling time of 2-3 days (Watanable *et al.,* 1977), quick decomposition in soil and efficient availability of its N to rice (Kannaiyan, 1990).

Mechanism of N-Fixation

Anabaena azollae present in the cavity of *Azolla* possess a multienzyme system called nitrogenase which can break down the very stable dinitrogen molecule and reduce it to ammonia molecule with the aid of energy source and electrons. The enzyme nitrogenase is made up of two different proteins, the molybdenum iron protein and the iron-protein, both of which are oxygen labile. Nitrogenase is extremely sensitive to oxygen which causes rapid inactivation. Thus the enzyme must be protected from both atmospheric oxygen and intercellular oxygen produced by photosynthesis.

The heterocyst in *A. Azollae* is the actual site of N_2 fixation. The enzyme nitrogenase is present in heterocyst. The primary source of ATP for N_2 fixation is photosystem, the reductant comes from the oxidative pentose phosphate pathway. The newly fixed N is incorporated into glutamine.

Factors Affecting Growth of Azolla

Water is essentially required for the existence of the *Azolla.* It becomes fragile in the moist soil and dies after complete drying. A water depth of 5-10 cm is recommended (Ashton, 1974). *Azolla* requires all the essential plant nutrients which must be available in the water. Phosphorus is most important element that limits the growth of *Azolla* and a deficiency in P results in red colouration and curling of roots (Cohn and Renlund, 1953). Under favourable conditions, addition of one kg of P results in fixation of about 5-10 kg N. Cobalt and molybdenum are required for efficient functioning of the N-Fixing system. *Azolla* prefers a certain degree of shading during summer, it reaches its full at 25-50 per cent of full sun light.

When the fern and rice are grown together in a dual cropping sytem, *Azolla* growth is below its potential due to shading by rice canopy which increases with advancing of rice growth (Singh, 1981). The growth and N-fixation are maximum at 20-30^{0}C, lower or higher temperature may decrease it growth and the fern dies when temperature is below 5^{0}C or above 45^{0}C (Lu *et al.,* 1963). The optimum pH for the growth of the fern is between 5.0 - 7.0 (Gowd *et al.,* 1980). The growth of *Azolla* is adversely affected by salinity, optimum salt concentration being 90--150 mg/litre. Nitrogen fertilizers usually affect adversely the growth of *Azolla*. *Azolla* is often attacked by insects and the entire crop is damaged within a few days if they are not tunely controlled.

Crop Response to Azolla

Azolla is either grown as green manure in fallow fields and incorporated before transplanting of rice or intercropped along with rice (Rains and Talley, 1979). Liu (1979) suggested that *Azolla* can be grown continuously in the rice fields by widening the distance between rice rows. The early inoculation of *Azolla* is favoured because less inoculum is required at the early stage of rice growth.

It is low cost bio-fertilizers which can contribute 30-60 kg N/ha/rice crop. Because of its rapid growth *Azolla* produces a good biomass in a short period. Within 20-30 days *Azolla* can multiply and produce biomass ranging from 15-25 t/ha. The nitrogen content is ranging from 3-5 per cent on dry weight basis. Azolla can easily be incorporated when rice crop is in the field and it decompases in the field rapidly and nitrogen is made available to rice plants. *Azolla* also controls weed flora in wetland rice.

Water is a pre-requisite for *Azolla*. It cannot be used in upland rice. The initial *Azolla* inoculum requirement as fresh biomass is 500-1000 kg/ha. Therefore, fresh *Azolla* inoculum is to be maintained in nursery plots throughout the year. The development of *Azolla* spore inoculants is under intensive field study and its success would eliminate the use of large fresh biomass for initial inoculum. *Azolla* twice intercropping in addition to its basal incorporation increased the yield of rice more than applying 60 kg N/ha as urea.

Blue Green Algae

The Organism

Ever since De (1939) attributed the inherent fertility of the tropical rice field soils to the activity of nitrogen fixing blue-green algae, considerable interest has been generated in exploiting the potential of these biological systems. BGA are photosynthetic nitrogen fixers *i.e.* they use energy derived from photosynthesis to fix atmospheric nitrogen. They are also called cynobacteria and are free living organisms. The principal genera consisting of maximum number of nitrogen fixing species are *Aulosira, Nostac, Anabaena, Tolypothrix, Scytonema, Plectonema* and *Cylindrospermum* (Kaushik, 1958). Contrary to general belief that BGA are present invariably in tropical rice soils, the distribution of soils harbouring N-fixing BGA varies from as low as 4 per cent to as high as 80 per cent (Sankaram, 1971), species of *Nostoc* and *Anabaena* were ubiquitous in all regions and formed the major constituent of the algae biotype (Venkataraman, 1988). An all India survey has indicated that out of 2,213 soil samples examined, only 33 per cent were found to contain useful N-fixing BGA (Kaushik, 1985). This indicates the need for inoculation of efficient strain of BGA.

Currently, the technology for mass production of soil-based algae inoculations is well developed and in active use in India. Four common methods of algal production are: through method, Pit method, Field method and Nursery method. The basic principle is to grow them in natural sunlight under conditions stimulating those in the rice field (Kaushik 1990). Sun dried algal material can be stored for long and used in the field.

Factors Affecting Growth and N-fixation by BGA

Most BGA prefer 5-10 cm standing water for their growth (Singh. 1985). Alternate wetting and drying of paddy fields encourage BGA growth (Kolte and Goyal, 1989). Although low light intensities are generally preferred, certain forms can grow well under high light intensities (Singh, 1976). The paddy water itself is a good temperature conditioner hence BGA will rarely be limited by any violent temperature extremes in lowland rice fields (Roger and Reynaud, 1979). The optimum pH for BGA range from 7.5 to 10. BGA are relatively salt solerant (Venkataraman, 1988) and have been used in reclamation of alkali soils (Singh, 1961). Predators and pathogens limit BGA growth and may cause rapid death of large BGA blooms (Daft and Stewart, 1971). Phosphorus is the primary growth limiting nutrient which should be present in available form in the food water. The minimum Mo level for BGA growth is 0.2 ppm. Addition of calcium carbonate enhance their growth and N-fixation. Inoculations of fresh BGA is better than dry BGA. Fresh BGA at 30-60 kg/ha and dry BGA at 3-10 kg/ha is recommended. Higher inoculum helps to cover paddy fields early. Fields are inoculated one week after transplanting preferably in morning hours to permit exposure to longer duration of sunlight. BGA growth is more in line planting than randomly planted or direct seeded rice.

Crop Response to BGA

The nitrogen fixed by BGA are released through exudation or through microbial decomposition after cells die. Comparison of N-fertilizer and BGA indicates that BGA inoculation is equivalent to the application of 20-30 kg N/ha (FAI, 1994). Grain yield measurement suggest that algalization produces a residual effect (Tirol *et al.,* 1982). Besides nitrogen, these algae are known to provide growth promoting substances (Gupta and Shukla, 1967). BGA incorporation improves carbon and nitrogen levels in the soil and promotes aggregation. The most frequently used criterion for assessing the effects of algalization has been better grain yield. The yield improvement due to algalization has been reported to vary from 15-28 per cent (Roger and Zkulasooriya, 1980).

Phosphate Solubilising Micro-Organisms

The Organisms

Phosphorus is the 'master key' element in crop production. The problems of P fertilization may become serious in coming years because of the fact that manufacture of phosphatic fertilizers require the use of non-renewable resources such as high grade rock phosphate and sulphur which are getting depleted progressively and becoming costlier. Crop yields would be limited by the rate at which phosphate is released from insoluble forms in the soil. The situation is further aggravated by the fact that P is readily fixed in the soil and the average utilization efficiency of added fertilizer P by plants ranges from 15-25 per cent (Kanwar *et al.,* 1972). Many soil micro-organisms have the capacity to solubilise insoluble inorganic phosphates known to occur in soil which include bacteria, fungi, actinomy cetes, yeast etc.

Mechanism of Phosphate Solubilisation

The production of organic acids like acetic, lactic, oxalic, citric etc. by PSM around plant roots is the most important cause of P solubilisation. These acids not only lower the pH but also help in the formation of stable complexes with P fixing ions like Ca, Mg, Fe and Al, thereby releasing P for plant use. Some PSM produce inorganic acids like nitric and sulphuric acids which react with insoluble forms of P and solubilise them (Somani *et al.,* 1990). The carbondioxide produced by PSM also help solubilise insoluble P (Stoklasa and Ernest, 1908). Hydrogen sulphide produced by sulphate reducing bacteria reduces ferrice phosphate (insoluble) to ferrous sulphate releasing soluble P (Patrick *et al.,* 1973). It is possible that PSM produce effective chelating compounds close to rock phosphate or fertilizer material and help solubilise P.

Factors Affecting P Solubilisation

PSM being heterotrophs, energy source play a vital role in secretion of organic acids to solubilise P (Ahmed and Jha, 1968). Nitrogen is needed for synthesis of animo acids and proteins by PSM. Different PSM have different preference for nitrogen source NH_4-N, NO_2-N, NO_3-N. The availability of preferred source affects P solubilisation (Gaur, 1985). Bacteria prefer neutral to slight acidic condition while fungi and yeast prefer a pH range of 4-6 (Swaby and Sperbes, 1958). The activity of PSM is adversely affected at low as well as high temperatures, the optimum being 20-40^{0}C (Gaur, 1985). The solubilisation is affected by kind of substrate. Tricalcium phosphate, hydroxy aptite, iron phsopahte and aluminium phosphates are effectively solubilised while rock phosphate is slowly solubilised (Gaur, 1983). Solubilisation of rock phosphate is also affected by chemical composition, concentration of P and particle size as well.

Crop Response to PSM

The use of PSM culture like phosphobacterin consisting of *Bacoillus megatorium* var *Phosphaticum* is an established practice in Russia and East European countries where yield increases of upto 70 per cent have been reported (Gaur, 1990). *Pseudomonas striata* has been found to increase the efficiency of superphosphate utilisation and yield of potato (Kundu and Gaur, 1980b). In some cases the release of growth stimulating substances produced by PSM has been found to be associated with enhanced uptake of micronutrients besides inhibiting the growth of fungal pathogen like *Fusarium* and *Alternaria* (Gaur, 1990).

Vesicular Arbuscular Mycorrhizae (VAM)

The Organism

It is widely known today that the roots of most flowering plants live associated, in a form of mutualistic symbiosis, with certain soil fungi by establishing the so called mycorrhizae. The fungus biotrophically colonisers the root cortex, becoming an integral part of these organs, where an extramatricial mycelium develops that help the plant acquire mineral nutrients from the soil. The symbiosis is considered the most metabolically active part of the absorbing organs of the autotrophic host plant, which in turn furnish the heterotrophic fungal associate with organic nutrients and with an ecologically protected habitat (Barga and Azcon-Aguilar, 1983). The mycorrhizae are of different types, the best known being the VAM which is characterised by the formation of branched haustorial structures (arbuscules) within the cortex cells and by a mycellium which extends well into the surrounding soil. The arbuscules are short lived (10-12 days), and are the main sites of solute exchange with the host. The ecological and economical interest of VAM can be simply deduced from the fact that about 80 per cent of land plants, including agronomicaly important crops, form this type of mycorrhizae.

Mechanism P Availability to Plants

VAM fungi is known to take up, accumulate and transfer large amounts of phosphate to the plants by releasing the nutrient in the root cells containing arbuscules. The fungal hyphae possibly produce organic acids such as citrate which solubilise phosphate. It is also possible that under conditions of P deficiency, the activity of certain enzymes produced by the fungi - the acid phosphatase - is enhanced transforming insoluble organic P into soluble orthophosphate. Since P is immobile in the soil, a zone of P-depletion develops around roots in P-deficient soils as roots absorb

P ions much faster than they can be replenished by diffusion. The VAM hyphae attached to the roots extend beyond the P-depletion zone and directly translocate nutrients over large distances from soil to the roots (Reid, 1979). Once inside the hyphae, phosphate is protected from refixation by soil components. The phosphate absorbed by VAM fungi from soil solution is accumulated in the vacuoles as polyphosphate granules which are propelled through the hyphae by cytoplasmic streaming (Cox and Tinker, 1976). Estimates show that the inflow of P through external hyphae is about 1,000 fold faster than the phosphate diffusion through soil pores (Bieleski, 1973). The polyphosphate granules in arbuscules are broken down by specific enzymatic activities releasing orthophosphate into the cytoplasm (Capacio and Callow, 1982).

Factors Affecting VAM Growth

The overall growth response of the plant of VAM is determined by a three way interaction among soil, plant and fungus. VAM formation is favoured by low to moderate soil fertility levels. Excess water, low oxygen levels and reducing conditions inhibit mycorrhizal formation (Reid, 1979). Some plant species and even cultivars are more dependent on mycorrhiza than others (Lambert *et al.,* 1980). Crops such as wheat with extensive fine root system, are not expected to respond to VAM except in P-deficient soil (Baylis, 1972). Lack of suitable host plants and/or long-term following can reduce the indigenous population of VAM fungi because these fungi are obligate symbiont. VAM fungal population can be increased by appropriate rotation or intercropping. Some other fungi may colonise the spores of VAM fungi. These hyperparasites limits the population of VAM fungi. A close correlation has been found between the effectiveness of the fungal species and the percentage of root length infected at early stages of plant growth. A decrease in light result in less photosynthesis and hence less carbohydrate available to the fungus to provide energy for nutrient uptake and nutrient transfer (Hayman, 1974). Low temperature may cause the endophyte to change from beneficial to mildly parasitic. Several biocidal fumigants are known to reduce mycorrhizal infection. The germination of spores of VA endophyte is sensitive to metals (Marx *et al.*, 1978).

Crop Response to VAM

Trials conducted with the locally isolated *Glomus macrocarpum* on chilli showed the possibility of saving 50 per cent phosphatic fertilizer without affecting the yield levels (Venkataraman and Tilak, 1990). The major constraint for field trials with VAM has been the inability to produce pure inoculum on a large scale as the fungi are obligate symbiont and have to be maintained and multiplied on living host plants (Janardhanan *et al.,* 1990).

Summary and Conclusion

The major nutrients inputs in crop cultivation, whether for fuel, fodder or food, are N and P. Nitrogen is free in the atmosphere and has to be in a fixed from to be made use of as a plant nutrient. Chemical fixation by way of combining elemental N and H to ammonia is highly expensive whereas biological fixation mediated by several free living micro-organisms and plant-microorganisms association through the enzyme nitrogenase is also energy requiring but does not deplete fossil fuels and hence has become really relevant to developing countries where major constraints on the farm inputs exist. Superphosphate or rock phosphate sources are meagre and many species of micro-organisms either solubilize bound phosphates in the rhizosphere or like the mycorrhizal fungi, serve to transport phosphorus into the plant system. Bio-fertilizers in a need of time.

References

FAI, 1994. *Bio-fertilizers in Indian Agriculture*. FAI, New Delhi.

Gaur A.C., 1990. *Phosphate Solubilizing Micro-organisms as Bio-fertilizers*. Omega Scientific Publishers, New Delhi.

Kannaiyan, S., 1990. *Biotechnology of Bio-fertilizers for Rice Crop*. TNAU, Coimbatore.

Somani, L.L. *et al.,* 1990. *Bio-fertilizers*. Scientific Publishers, Jodhpur.

Somani, L.L., 1987. *Bio-fertilizers in Indian Agriculture*. Concept Publishing Co., New Delhi.

Tandon, H.L.S., 1992. *Fertilizers, Organic Manures, Recyclable Wastes and Bio-fertilizers*, FDCO, New Delhi.

Tilak, K.V.B.R., 1991. *Bacterial Fertilizers*. ICAR, New Delhi.

Chapter 3

Use of Land as per Its Capabilities to Get Higher Production

R.L. Shyampura

Principal Scientist & Head, National Bureau of Soil Survey and Land Use Planning, RCA Campus, Udaipur

Introduction

Using of land according to its capability is possible by grouping the land units into defined classes. It is a broad grouping of soils based on their limitations and is designed to emphasise the hazards in different kinds of soils. It serves as a guide to assess suitability of the land for arable crops, grazing and forestry.

Land Capability Assessment

Klingebiel and Montgomery (1961) discussed the criteria for placing soils in different capability classes. The criteria used in assessing a land unit are the physical land properties and the degree of limitation as a function of the severity with which crop growth is inhibited. It is mainly based on (a) the inherent soil characteristics, (b) the external land features, and (c) the environmental factors that limit land use.

The capability classification consists of three categories, namely:

(i) capability classes,

(ii) capability subclasses,

(iii) capability units

The criteria used the group soils into different capability classes (Table 1) is qualitative and works well for new areas being brought under agricultural use. However, it may not be satisfactory for traditionally cultivated areas; such as Indo-Gangetic and Mesopotamia plains. Therefore, it needs quantification.

Table 1

Salient Features of Land Capability Classes

Land Suitable for Cultivation	
Class-I (green)	Very good cultivable, deep, nearly level, productive land with almost no limitation (or very slight hazard). Soils in this class are suited for a variety of crops, including wheat, barley, cotton, maize, tomato and bean. Need no special management practices for cultivation; shown as green on maps.
Class-II (yellow)	Good cultivable land on almost level plain or on gentle slopes that have slight limitations of soil depth, salinity, texture, drainage or erosion that reduce the choice of plants. In general, these soils are suitable for wheat, barley, cotton; moderately suitable for maize, alfalfa, tomato; and slightly-suitable for beans. Recommendation is to cultivate with precaution; need simple management practices; shown as yellow on maps.
Class-III (brown)	Moderately- good cultivable land on almost level plain or on moderate slope. These soils have limitation(s) of moderate erosion, soil depth, soil salinity, soil texture. They have vertic characteristics or drainage problem that reduces the choice of crop. In general, these areas have varying suitability for different crops. They are unsuitable for growing vegetable crops. Recommendation is to cultivate with careful management practices; need intensive care; shown as brown on maps.
Class-IV (pink)	Fairly-good land on almost level plains or moderately-steep slopes. Suitable for occasional or limited cultivation; generally unsuitable for growing a variety of crops because of strong or very strong soil salinity (S3/S4), shallow depth, erosion, fine texture or poor or excessive drainage. Suitable for selected crops and for pasture. Such soils may not be economical to cultivate as they need intensive soil conservation and management practices; shown as pink on maps.

Land Unsuitable for Cultivation but Suitable for Permanent Vegetation (Grazing)

Class-V (dark grey)	Land not suitable for arable farming, but very suitable for grazing; have limitations for use of implements due to stony or rocky and marshyness; shown as dark grey on maps.
Class-VI (orange)	Non-arable land, well suited for grazing or forestry use. Have moderate limitations, such as steep slope, severe erosion, limited soil depth, strongly gypsiferous, stony or sand-dune areas. For instance, the dense forest lands of the Himalayas (India) or gypsiferous and dunal areas of SW Iraq; shown as orange on maps.
Class-VII (red)	Fairly-well suited for grazing or forestry; not cultivable. Have severe limitations, such as very steep land subjected to erosion or very shallow, stony soils having not enough available moisture for cultivation. Need careful management for grazing and forestry; shown as red on maps.
Class-VIII (purple)	Non-arable, extremely rough, rocky, arid, wet or extremely saline land, suited only for wild life or recreation. Have very severe limitation, for instance highly eroded land, barren mountain tops (as in the Himalayas) or rocky undulating surfaces (as in desert of south-western Iraq), shown as purple on map.

Land Capability Subclass

It provides information as to the kind of conservation problems or limitation involved, within Land capability class based on the wetness (w); climate (c); soil (s); and erosion (e).

Capability Units

The capability subclasses are further sub-divided into units including soils those are sufficiently uniform in their characteristics, potential and limitation and require fairly uniform conservation treatments and management practices.

Land Suitability Evaluation

The minimum data base needed for land evaluation towards the land use planning (Ingram. 1993) are given in table-2. Based on these parameters various scheme of land evaluation is proposed store (1954), and Ricquier *et al.* (1970). The F.A.O. panels for land evaluation (1976) defined the concept of land utilisation types and suggested the classification of land for specific use.

Table 2

Minimum Data Set Needed for Land Evaluation for Land Use Planning

Primary Data Set	
Profile (as a whole)	*Upper Each Horison*
• Site (latitude & longitude) • Site slope and aspect • Landscape position • Parent materials • Current land use, and nutrient input (kg ha-1 yr-1) • Soil depth • FAO/USDA soil classifications • Local soil series ration (SAR) • Structural class • Presence/absence of roots • Occurrence of mottle or gleying	• Upper and lower depths (cm) • Bulk density • % stone content • Particle size classes • Organic C • CEC • % base saturation • pH (H_2O) or pH (CaC12) • Electrical conductivity • Sodium absorption
Additional Data Set	*Existing Data Set*
• Water-table • Water-logging (duration) • Bulk density	• Climate • Soil biology • Vegetation
Derived Data Set	
Basic data	*Derived data*
• CEC, OM, clay • Rooting depth, mineralogy texture • Base saturation, CEC • pH , SAR, ESP • C, N bulk density, kind of vegetation	• Mineralogy • Av. Water holding capacity • Acidity • Alkalinity • C and N stocks

The land suitability unit is used to identify land development unit having minor differences in the management requirements. This suggests the relative importance of land improvement works.

Evaluation of Soils of Rajasthan for District Land Use Planning

Characterisation of Agro-Ecological Zones of Rajasthan

Rajasthan with 34.2 m ha geographical area have 31 agro-ecological zones (Fig.1). Each AEZ is uniform with respect to length of growing period (LGP), land from and soil characteristics (Table 3). Wide variability with respect to rainfall (100 mm to 1000 mm), LGP (<45 to 150 days), texture (coarse sandy to massive clay), depth (skeletal soil to >125 cm) affect land use and choice of crops, grasses and trees. Limited rainfall and LGP (<75 days) in 45.6 per cent of the area in association with sandy soils with severe erosion (40.2%), salinity (10.8%) and shallow skeletal soils (9.6%) are major limiting factors affecting choice in land use.

Table 3

Land Use Suitability Characteristics of Agro-Ecological Zones of Rajasthan

AEZ	*LGP (days)*	*Depth (cm)*	*Texture*	*Erosion*	*EC (dSm)*	*Area ('000 ha)*
1	90-105	25-50	Loamy sk.*	Severe	-	1388.2
2	90-105	50-75	Loamy	Moderate	-	971.3
3	90-105	> 100	Sandy	Moderate	-	296.1
4	90-105	50-75	Loamy	Moderate	-	1324.0
5	120-135	50-75	Loamy	Moderate	-	921.5
6	90-105	75-100	Loamy	Slight	-	201.6
7	105-120	75-100	Loamy	Slight	-	4462.9
8	105-120	> 100	Loamy	Severe	-	158.5
9	90-103	> 100	Sandy	Moderate	-	221.3
10	90-105	> 100	Loamy	Moderate	-	402.9
11	105-120	< 25	Loamy sk.	Severe	-	992.5
12	105-120	> 100	Loamy	Moderate	-	379.3
13	105-120	> 100	Loamy	Slight	-	278.7

14	105-120	> 100	Loamy	Severe	-	645.7
15	105-120	> 100	Clayey	Severe	-	593.8
16	135-150	50-75	Loamy sk.	Severe	-	919.4
17	135-150	75-100	Clayey	Severe	-	194.0
18	< 45	75-100	Loamy	Moderate	-	349.5
19	< 45	75-100	Sandy	Moderate	-	1194.0
20	< 45	> 100	Loamy	Moderate	4-8	714.0
21	< 45	> 100	Sandy	Severe	-	3490.7
22	45-60	50-75	Loamy	Severe	4-8	1476.6
23	45-60	> 100	Loamy	Moderate	4-8	1556.4
24	45-60	> 100	Sandy	Severe	-	3456.0
25	60-75	> 100	Sandy	Severe	-	1187.9
26	60-75	> 100	Sandy	Moderate	-	733.2
27	45-60	>125	Loamy	Moderate	-	1273.5
28	45-60	> 100	Clayey	Slight	-	196.1
29	75-90	50-75	Loamy	Moderate	-	1296.3
30	75-90	> 100	Sandy	Moderate	-	1432.1
31	75-90	> 100	Loamy	Severe	-	369.6

*Sk: Skeletal with gravel >40%.

Suitability of Soils

Thirty-one delineated agroecological zone (AEZ) of Rajasthan were evaluated for suitability for rainfed crops (maize, sorghum, pearlmillet, clusterbean and moth), grasses (Lasiurus sindicus, Cenchrus sp., Dicanthium annulatum) and tree plantation (17 tree species suitable for fuel wood, wind break, shelter belt, fodder species, agroforestry). Based on limitations of rainfall, LGP, depth, texture, salinity, surface condition the suitability class for each crop, grass and tree species were adjudged for its productivity at given level of individual parameter as following:

Suitable	S1	:	85% productivity
Moderately Suitable	S2	:	60% productivity
Marginally Suitable	S3	:	40% productivity
Not Suitable	N	:	<40% productivity

Overall suitability of AEZ for crop, grass and trees were determined on the basis of following criterion:

Suitable : One limitation of S2 level

Moderately Suitable : Two limitations of S2 or one major limitation of S3

Marginally Suitable : Three limitations of S2 level or two limitations of S3 level or one limitation of N level

Not Suitable : Three limitations of S3 level or two limitations of N level

Suitability of agro-ecological zones of Rajasthan for crop, grasses and tree species are given in Table 4.

Table 4

Suitability of Agro-Ecological Zones of Rajasthan for Different Land Use

AEZ	*Crops*		*Grass*		*Trees*	
	S1	***S2***	***S1***	***S2***	***S1***	***S2***
1	-	-	CC	DA		-
2	P, S, M	C	DA	CC	4, 5, 9-12	1, 2, 4, 6, 13, 15-17
3	P, S, M	C	CC	LS	3-12, 15	1, 2, 13, 14, 16, 17
4	P, S, M	C	CC	DA	3, 5, 8-12	1, 2, 4, 6, 7, 13, 15, 17
5	P, S, M	C	DA	CC	13, 17	8-12, 14-16
6	P, S, M, C	-	CC	DA	2-6, 8-13, 17	1, 7, 14, 16
7	P, S, M	C	CC	DA	8-13, 15, 17	1-7, 14, 16
8	-	P, S, M	DA	CC	8, 10-15, 17	1-7, 9, 16
9	P	S, M, C	CC	-	3-12	1, 2, 13-17
10	P, S, M, C,	-	CC	DA	1-13, 15, 17	14, 16
11	-	-	DA	CC	-	–
12	S, M	-	DA	CC	8-17	1-7
13	S, M	P	DA	CC	8-17	1-7

14	-	P, S, M	DA	CC	8, 10-15, 17	1-7, 9
15	-	S, M	DA	CC	-	3-5, 8, 10-15
16	-	-	DA	CC	-	-
17	-	S, M	DA	CC	-	13, 14, 17
18	Mo	C	LS	CC	-	1-7
19	Mo	P, C	LS	CC	-	2-7
20	-	C, Mo	LS	CC	-	1-7
21	-	Mo	LS	CC	-	3-7
22	-	P, Mo	LS	CC	5	3, 4, 8
23	Mo	P, C	LS	CC	2, 4, 5	1, 3, 6-9
24	-	P, C, Mo	LS	CC	3-5	6-9
25	-	P, C, Mo	LS	CC	3-8	1, 2, 9
26	C, Mo	P	LS	CC	1-9	10-12
27	C, Mo	P	LS, CC	-	1-7	8, 9
28	-	P, C	CC	DA	-	1-9
29	P	S, C	CC	DA	2-6, 8, 9	1, 7, 10-13, 16, 17
30	P, C, Mo	-	CC	LS	1-9	10-13, 15, 17
31	S, M	P, S, M, C	CC, DA	-	1-9	10-13, 15, 17

Suitability: S1-suitable; S2-moderately suitable

Crops: P-Pearlmillet; S-Sorghum; M-Maize; C-Clusterbean; Mo-Moth

Grasses: CC-Cenchrus species; DA-Dicanthium annulatum; LS-Lasiurus sindicius

Tree: 1. Acacia albida 2. A. nilotica 3. A. senegal 4. A. tortilis 5. Prosopis juliflora 6. P. cineraria 7. Tecomella undulata 8. Parkinsonis aculeate 9. Salvadora oleoides 10. Albizzia lebbek 11. Colophosperum mopane 12. Dichrystachys nutan 13. Cassia siamea 14. Casuarina equistefolia 15. Eucalyptus camaldulensis 16. E. tereticornis 17. Leucaena leucocephala

Crops

Pearl millet, sorghum and maize are suitable and moderately suitable for AEZ in hot semi arid aravalli ecosystem (14.3%) and eastern Rajasthan uplands (12.9%). Pearl millet, cluster bean and moth are suitable for AEZ in hyper arid western Rajasthan (25.3%)

and aeolin plain (3.5%). In hot semi arid aeoflurial lunibanin (12.3%) pearlmillet, sorghum, maize and clusterbean area suitable/moderately suitable.

Figure 1

Rajasthan: Agro Ecological Zones

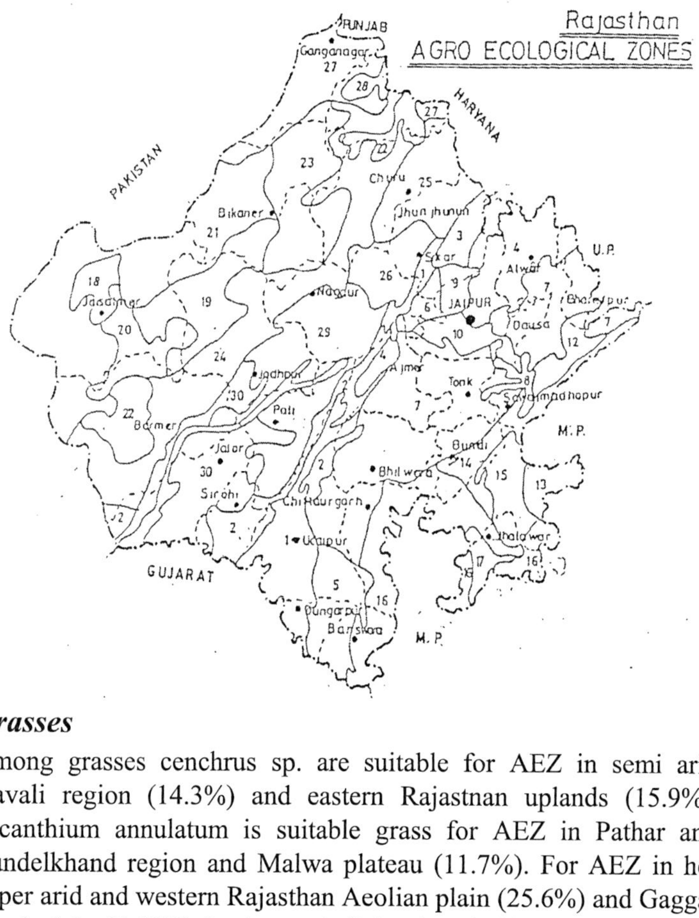

Grasses

Among grasses cenchrus sp. are suitable for AEZ in semi arid aravali region (14.3%) and eastern Rajastnan uplands (15.9%). Dicanthium annulatum is suitable grass for AEZ in Pathar and Bundelkhand region and Malwa plateau (11.7%). For AEZ in hot hyper arid and western Rajasthan Aeolian plain (25.6%) and Gaggar flood plain (6.43%) Lasiurus sindicius is suitable grass. Cenchrus sp. and Dicanthium annulatum are suitable grass for AEZ in aeofluvial Luni basin (12.3%).

Trees

Among trees Acacia albida, A. nilotica, A. tortilis, A. senegal, Prosopis juliflera, P. cineraria, Tecomella undulata are suitable to moderately suitable for AEZ in hot hyper arid and aeolian plain (25.6%) and suitable for semi arid aeolin plain (9.2%), Gaggar flood plain and Luni basin area (12.3%). AEZ in Aravalli region are suitable for Albizzia lebbek, Colophospermum mopane, Dichrystachys mutan. AEZ in eastern Rajasthan upland are suitable for Eucalyptus camaldulensis, E. tereticornis, Casuarina equestefloia, AEZ with skeletal soils (9.6%) are only marginally suitable for tree plantations.

Land Use Priorities

Extent of area under different suitability class for crops, grass and trees are given in table 5. Overall suitability of soils of Rajasthan for different crops, grass and tree was calculated by summation of product of percent area in each suitability class with productivity potential of each class. (S1- 0.85; S2-0.6; S3-0.4; N-0.2).

Overall suitability= E% area × productivity potential

Table 5

Suitability of Soils of Rajasthan for Different Land Use

(Area '000 ha)

Land Use	Suitable	Moderately Suitable	Marginally Suitable	Not Suitable	Suitability Index
Crops					
Pearl millet	12630	12906	6334	2307	62.8
Sorghum	9238	4580	7378	12982	47.2
Maize	9238	2177	9331	13425	45.8
Cluster bean	3943	19616	5883	7434	54.0
Moth	9131	10323	10264	4457	-
Grass					
Lasiurus sindicus	13874	1728	8972	9503	53.6
Cenchrus sp.	13963	20114	-	-	70.0
Dicanthium annulatum	6425	7660	296	19696	41.3

Trees					
Acacia albida	4211	15340	12714	1912	53.4
A. nilotica	8366	12379	12440	992	57.5
A. Senegal	14260	15496	4416	-	67.8
A. Tortilis	13527	16235	3423	992	69.4
Prosopis Juliflera	17299	12463	4415	-	70.0
P. Cineraria	8515	19177	5494	992	61.8
Tecomella undulata	5917	21775	4574	1912	51.7
Parkinsonia aculeate	15461	8880	9202	-	60.5
Salvadora oleoides	13469	9396	11013	-	63.2
Albizzia lebbek	9342	6446	18330	-	55.5
Colophospermum mopane	9342	6446	18330	-	55.5
Dichrystachys nutan	9342	6446	18330	-	55.5
Cassia siamea	7451	7798	18928	-	52.5
Casuaria equistefolia	1462	6294	24033	1388	45.3
Eucalyptus camaldulensis	6845	5814	20042	1477	51.5
E. Tereticornis	658	7311	23829	2387	43.7
Leucaena leucocephala	7451	7798	18928	-	52.5

Geographical area of Rajasthan 34247 ('000 ha).

Among rainfed crops maximum area of Rajasthan (36.9%) is suitable for pearlmillet follwed by sorghum, maize, moth and cluster bean. Overall suitability of rainfed crops is in order pearlmillet-moth-clusterbean-sorghum-maize. Among grasses Cenchrus sp. and lasiurus sindicus are suitable for 40 per cent area. Overall suitability is in order Cenchrus sp.- Lasiurus sindicus - Dicanthium annulatum. Among trees Prosopis cineraria, P. juliflera, Acacia Senegal, A. tortilis, Parkinsonia acuraeta are suitable for fuelwood, shelter belt and wind break plantation. Among commercial plantation Eucalyptus camaldulensis is most suitable. For crops excessive rainfall is major limitation for cluster bean, pearlmillet and moth. Moisture deficiency is major limitation for maize and sorghum. On the basis of suitability of crops, grasses and trees for agroecological zones appropriate choice can be made depending upon regional and farmers priorities for optimal land use and sustained productivity.

References

Annual Report (1998). NBSS & LUP, Regional Centre, Udaipur.

FAO (1976). "A frame work for Land Evaluation" *Soil Bull.* 32, FAO, Rome.

Ingram, J. (1993). "IGBP-DIS working Paper 7," In IBGP-DIS/GCTE Global Soil data base workshop held at Silsoe (U.K.) Oct. 1992.

Keingebiel A. A. and P.H. Montgomery (1961). *Land capability classification USDA Handbook.* 210. SCS. U. S. Govt. Pr. Office, Washington, D. C. 21 p.

Ricqueer, J. D.L. Bramao and J.P. Cornet (1970). "A new system of soil appraisel in terms of actual and potential productivity." *Soil Resour. Dev. And Consery. Service* FAO. Rome.

Sehgal J.L. (1995). "Land Resources Appraisal for Land use Planning to Meet the challenges of 21st century" *J. Indian Soc. Soil Sci.* 43 (4): 504-528.

Sehgal J.L. (1996).: *Pedology-concepts and application*, p. 251: Kalyani Publishers Ludhiana India.

Storie, R.E. (1154). "Land Classification used in California." 5th Int. Soil Conf. Leopotdvele III: 407-412.

Chapter 4

Organic Matter Recycling for Plant Nutrients

S.C. Bhandari

Dept. of Agri. Chem. & Soil Sciences, RCA, Udaipur

Introduction

Soil organic matter is an essential component of soil although it varies from negligible in desert soils to as much as 95 per cent in some peat soils. Plant may complete its life-cycle with the supply of all essential nutrients as in case of hydroponics, but when grown in soil, the soil humus which is derived from the plant and animal residues, contributes significantly to growth and yield of plants by improving physical, chemical and biological properties and helps in sustaining the agriculture. Organic matter is an important component of natural farming and ancestors had agriculture on natural resources. With the introduction of chemical fertilizers and quick visible response of crops to its application, the emphasis had tilted in favour of fertilizers especially nitrogenous ones in the recent past. On the other hand, the recycling of organic wastes to fields reduced greatly on account of its alternate use as fuel in rural areas which was a compulsion as no substitute was available.

Composition of Organic Matter

Organic matter recycled into the soil may have the origin from plants, animals and micro-organisms. Plants contribute in the form of left over roots, fallen leaves and twigs and residues recycled after harvest. Animals contribute through excretion and dead bodies. Micro-organisms and soil organism contribute through carbon fixation and auto death. Chemically all these sources have carbohydrates, proteins, lipids, waxes, pigments minerals etc. These may not act as direct source of nutrients but on decomposition which is dominantly a microbiological process along with physical and chemical processes, release nutrients which are utilised by plants. This process is continuous and soil has original residues, metabolic products, secondary metabolic products, humus etc. at a particular time. The proportion of different components in sources varies with age, so also its rate of decomposition. The ratios of C:N, C:P and C:S increases with the age of plants. Different groups of chemical components present in organic sources are given in Table 1 and the range of different component are given in Table 2. The ratio of C:N of different sources are given in Table 3. It indicates the variability among the sources.

Table 1

Chemical Composition of Organic Sources

S. No.	*Class*	*Sub-classes*
1.	Protein	Albumin, histone, protamin, globulin, prolamine, glulelein, keratin.
2.	Lipids	Triglycerides, sterols, waxes, phospholipids Monosacchorides, disaccharides.
3.	Carbohydrates	Polysaccharides, chitin, mucopolysaccharides, heteropolysaccharides.
4.	Conjugated compounds	Nucleoproteins, chromoproteins, Lipoproteins, phosphoproteins, flavoproteins, glycoproteins, adipocellulose.

Table 2

Range of Different Groups of Bio-Molecules in Plants

S. No.	*Bio-Molecules*	*Range (%)*
1.	Cellulose	15-60
2.	Hemicellulose	10-50
3.	Lignin	5-30
4.	Water soluble	5-30
5.	Fats, Oils, Wax and Resins	0.5-5
6.	Protein	5-10
7.	Minerals	1-13

Table 3

C:N Ratio of Different Organic Sources

S. No.	*Organic Source*	*C:N Ratio*
1.	Maize	38 : 1
2.	Wheat	60 : 1
3.	Alfalfa (young)	13 : 1
4.	Clover	20 : 1
5.	Bluegrass	30 : 1
6.	Straw, small grains	80 : 1
7.	Saw dust	225 : 1
8.	Bacteria	5 : 1
9.	Actinomycetes	6 : 1
10.	Fungi	10 : 1
11.	Soil humus	11 : 1

Role of Organic Matter

Organic matter, irrespective of source, on incorporation contributes to beneficial and/or detrimental effect. It may vary and extensive as well.

Benefits:

1. It acts as a reservoir of plant nutrients and also prevents their losses.
2. It affects the availability of nutrients by evelation.
3. It helps in buffering capacity of soil.
4. It helps in maintaining soil structure.
5. It helps in transmission of heat.
6. It is source of carbon for helerotrophs.
7. It influences the efficiency of chemicals, their degradability and toxicity.
8. It helps plant through growth substances.
9. It reduces the toxicities of pollutants like heavy metals.
10. It conserves the soil and water.
11. It is a soil amendment.

Detrimental Effect

1. It may help in proliferation of pathogens.
2. Excessive organic residues may hinder tillage and planting operations.
3. It may influence through phytotoxins.
4. It may be detrimental due to allclochemicals.

Potential of Organic Nutrient Sources

With the increasing production of food, the demand for plant nutrients has increased and it will increase further in the time to come. The production in 1951-52 was 51.99 mt which increased to 185.05 mt in 1995-96 with a corresponding consumption of NPK to 65.6 and 13876.1 thousand tonnes (Anon., 1997). If we want to meet the targeted yield potential of the beginning of next century with available land under plough, we have to increase the input of nutrients as well as balance it (Dev, 1996). Looking to the limits of production of inorganic fertilizers, we have to exploit the available organic sources which may be in the forms of livestock wastes, crop residues, tree wastes, aquatic weeds, green manures etc. These are rich sources of plant nutrients. Vimal and Talashilkar (1983) had estimated that there was 13 mt of nutrients through organic wastes (Table 4) and part of it atleast can be recycled. It will not only solve the problem of macronutrients but also of secondary and micronutrients.

Table 4

Potential of Organic Resources as Plant Nutrients

Organic Resource	***Quantity (lac tones per year)***	***Nutrients ('000 tonnes)***			
		N	***P_2O_5***	***K_2O***	***Total***
Cattle dung and urine	12247.1	2977.0	793.0	1332.0	5102.0
Buffalo dung and urine	4367.7	745.0	276.0	487.0	1508.0
Other animal wastes	428.4	389.9	229.6	133.0	752.5
Crop	1599.5	810.9	562.7	2085.4	3459.0

Fruit and vegetables	0.3	0.2	0.1	0.2	0.5
Forest residues/waste	175.0	243.6	34.4	98.8	576.8
Human habitation waste	3194.8	815.5	322.1	248.8	1386.4
Aquatic biomass	30.0	60.0	30.0	60.0	150.0
Total	*22042.8*	*6042.1*	*2247.9*	*4445.2*	*12735.2*

Livestock Wastes

The livestock population of India has shown as increasing trend from 369.5 million in 1977 to 470.1 million in 1992 (Table 5). The amount of excretion from animals depends upon breed, age, weight, nutrition etc. and average excretions is given in Table 6. It is maximum in case of horse and minimum in case of sheep. Nutrient content of urine and excreta of selected animals are given in Table 7.

Table 5

India's Livestock Population ('000)

Animals	***Number of Animal***			
	1977	***1982***	***1987***	***1992***
Cattle	180140	192453	199695	204533
Buffaloes	62019	69783	75966	83499
Sheep	40907	48765	45703	50799
Goats	75620	95255	110207	115278
Horses and ponnies	916	900	797	826
Pigs	7647	10071	10625	12795
Mules	89	131	167	197
Donkeys	978	1024	958	970
Camels	1068	1078	1001	1035
Others	132	128	165	212
Total	*369526*	*419588*	*445284*	*470146*

Source: Anon (1997).

Table 6

Urine and Excreta Production by Some Animals (kg/year)

Animals	Average Weight (kg)	Dung	Urine	Total
Cow	250	6560	2000	8560
Ox	325	8750	2500	11250
Sheep	45	510	170	680
Pig	90	1020	405	1425
Horse	575	10200	2040	12240

Source: Vyas *et al.* (1996).

Table 7

Nutrient Content (%) of Fresh Excretions of Animals

Animal's Excretion	Dung	P_2O_5	K_2O
Dung of Cow and Ox	0.40	0.20	0.10
Urine of Cow and Ox	1.00	Trace	1.35
Dung of Sheep and Goat	0.75	0.50	0.45
Urine of Sheep and goat	1.35	0.05	2.10
Dung of Horse	0.55	0.30	0.40
Urine of Horse	1.35	Trace	1.25
Dung of Pig	0.55	0.50	0.40
Urine of Pig	0.40	0.10	0.45

Source: Vyas *et al.* (1996).

Gaur (1992) reported that annual excretion of wet dung and urine from cattle and buffalo worked out to be 1228 and 800 mt respectively with a potential of 3,442, 1,307 and 2,214 mt of N, P_2O_5 and K_2O. (Table 8). Based on rough estimates, Biswas *et al.* (1991) reported that out of this 75 per cent may be used as fuel while it was 30-50 per cent in 1970.

Table 8

Nutrient Content and Theoretical Potential of Total Dung and Urine Excretion by Cattle and Buffaloes

Source	Annual Excretions (mt)	Million Tonnes					
		N		P_2O_5		K_2O	
		%	mt	%	mt	%	mt
Wet dung	1227.8	0.15	1.842	0.10	1.227	0.05	0.614
Urine	800.0	0.20	1.600	0.01	0.080	0.20	1.600
Total NPK (mt)			*3.442*		*1.307*		*2.214*

Source: Gaur (1992).

Crop Residues

Large number of crops are grown and after making use of their economic part, remaining part is wasted except for a few crops. The potential of crop residues as source of nutrients is enormous. The farm residues and nutrient content of selected crops are given in Table 9. Nutrient from five major crops *viz.* paddy, wheat, pearl millet, sorghum and maize alone comes out to 1.13 mt N, 1.41 mt P_2O_5 and 3.54 mt K_2O and 50 per cent of it can be made available for recycling assuming equal amount is used as fodder.

Table 9

Potential of Farm Residues as Plant Nutrients

Crop	Grain: Straw Ratio	Residue (mt)	Percentage		
			N	P_2O_5	K_2O
Rice straw	1 : 1.5	106.01	0.58	0.23	1.66
Wheat straw	1 : 1.5	80.99	0.49	0.25	1.28
Sorghum	1 : 2.0	21.04	0.40	0.23	2.17
Pearl millet	1 : 2.0	15.58	0.65	0.75	2.50
Maize	1 : 1.5	12.50	0.59	0.31	1.31
Total pulses	1 : 1.0	13.70	1.60	0.15	2.00
Pigeonpea	1 : 2.5	6.65	1.10	0.58	1.28
Chickpea	1 : 1.0	5.05	1.19	-	1.25
Sugarcane	1 : 0.2	40.92	0.35	0.04	0.50
Oil Seeds	1 : 2.0	35.78	-	-	-

Source: Ministry of Finance 1990-91 & FAO *Field Document No. 15 & 24.*

Other Plant Wastes

In India, a number of weeks occupy considerable area that is not under cultivation. Water hyacinth in water bodies has been reported to occupy 292 thousand hectares and about 250 t/ha is the estimated biomass production per year showing the huge potential of it as organic source of nutrients. About 3 mt compost could be produced annually which will provide 20.5 Kg N, 11.0 Kg P_2O_5 and 25 Kg K_2O per tonne (Gaur *et al.*, 1984).

Other major weeds occupying non-cultivable areas in the country are Lantana camara, Eupatorium spp. And Parthenium which otherwise are of no use either as fuel or fodder. In addition, these weeds are responsible for health hazards to both animals and human beings. Studies have shown that Lantana and Eupatorium can be used as manure to supplement the nutrients either through composting or through direct incorporation in puddle rice. It is further estimated that about 15 million tonnes of compost can be obtained from forest litter annually without adversely affecting the natural regeneration of the forest. Fifteen million tonnes of forest litter manure may contain 0.075, 0.03, 0.075 million tonnes of N, P_2O_5, and K_2O respectively. At present, however, considerable amount of leaf litter is burnt and huge quantities of plant nutrients are wasted in the process.

The potential availability of rural and town compost is estimated to be 600 million and 15 million tonnes, respectively. If managed properly, rural compost may supply 3.0 million tonnes each of N and P_2O_5, and 3.5 million tonnes of K_2O. Urban compost will supply 0.22, 0.15 and 0.22 million tonnes of N, P_2O_5 and K_2O respectively. About 0.3 million tonnes of non-edible cake is produced annually which includes neem cake, karanj cake, mahua cake, and castor cake. The manurial value of these cakes is mainly because of their nitrogen content which varies from 3 to 9 per cent, depending upon the nature of cakes.

Availability of rice husk in India is about 15 million tonnes annually and it contains 0.3 to 0.4 per cent N, 0.2 to 0.3 per cent P_2O_5 and 0.3 to 0.5 per cent K_2O. There is a problem of its disposal in some areas. Its usefulness in composting may hold promise. Besides this, about 2 million tonnes of press mud is produced annually from the sugar factories in India. It contains about 1.25 per cent N and 2 per cent of P_2O_5. It is very high in line (45%) and, therefore, its application is useful in acidic soils. The total of saw dust wastes is estimated at about 2.2 million tonnes in the country. It has good liquid absorbing capacity and can absorb 2-4 times more moisture than cereal residues. It can be gainfully used as an absorbent for soaking urine in cattle sheds.

A large quantity of wastes are obtained in the form of peels, corns, pit wine, and other materials from vegetables and fruit processing plants. There is a wide scope for utilisation of these wastes as manure. The total quantity available from this industry is more than 25,000 tonnes from mango, pineapple, citrus, apples, green peas, tomato and other products annually. It is estimated that about 10,000 tonnes of compost could be produced out of these wastes if managed properly.

The total production of cotton stalks on all India basis is estimated at 12.0 million tonnes which are generally used for fuel purpose or burnt in the field for disposal. The alternate technology for covering it into manure needs, to be developed for adoption. Further, while processing, cotton textile mills mainly in their blowing rooms produce a large quantity of cotton dust. These mills in India are estimated to produce 30,000 to 33,000 tonnes of this waste per year, which contains 1.4 per cent N, 0.6 per cent P_2O_5 and 1.2 per cent K_2O and thus may be an important source to meet the nutrient requirements of the crops.

About 10 million kg of tea waste becomes available in the form of fluffs, stalks and sweepings. The decaffeinated tea waste can be used as a manure. Spent tea waste contents 0.28-0.35 per cent N, 0.4 per cent P_2O_5, and 1.51 per cent K_2O. Besides this, about 62,000 tonnes of tobacco waste is available annually. Tobacco waste contains 0.5 to 1.0 per cent N, 0.8 per cent P_2O_5, and 0.8 per cent K_2O. About 10,000 tonnes of tobacco seed cake is also available and it contains 4 to 4.5 per cent N, 7 to 15 per cent P_2O_5, and 5 to 5.5 per cent K_2O.

Use of Organic Wastes

The organic sources are carbonaceous materials having great variation in C:N ratio which determines the rate of decomposition, release of nutrients and also the duration for completion of composting process. The decomposition rate also depends on temperature; soil conditions, moisture, supplementation, inoculation etc. Basically there are two processes of narrowing the C:N ratio, first is *in situ* as in case of green manuring, fallen leaves and twigs etc. and second is *in vitro* in pits or trenches following different procedures as Bangalore, Indore, NADEP, vermicompost, mechanical compost etc which have been discussed elsewhere under composting and vermicomposting. The rate of composting can be accelerated by supplementing with chemicals and/or inoculum and have been discussed elsewhere under enriched compost.

Conclusion

Integrated use of organic sources with organic fertilizers is useful as it provides both macro and micronutrients and also improves the long-term productivity of soil through improvement in physical, chemical and biological properties. Looking to the quantum of organic wastes, there is good scope of recycling and to reduce dependence of chemical fertilizers.

References

Anon (1997) *Agricultural statistics at a glance*. Directorate of Economics and Statistics, Department of Agriculture and Cooperation, Govt. of India, New Delhi.

Biswas, B.C. *et al* (1991) *Fert. Mktg. News*, 22(8), 1.

Dev, G (1996) *Balanced fertilizer use for increasing foodgrains production in Western states*. PPIC, Gurgaon.

Gaur, A.C. (1992) In: *Fertilizers, Organic manures, recyclable wastes and bio-fertilizers* (Ed. H.L.S. Tandon), FDCO, New Delhi.

Gaur, A.C., Neelakantan, S. and Dargan, K.S. (1984). *Organic manures*, ICAR, New Delhi.

Vimal, O.P. and Talashilkar, S. (1983). *J. Sci. Ind. Res.* 42:115.

Vyas, K.K., Bhandari, S.C. and Singh S.D. (1996) *Mrida Vigyan*, Rajasthan Hindi Granth Academy, Jaipur.

Chapter 5

Biogas Slurry: A Source of Plant Nutrients & Its Management

Dr. A.N. Mathur

College of Tech. & Agri. Engineering, Udaipur

Introduction

The foodgrain production in the country which was 50 million tonnes during 1947 has reached to 187 million tonnes by the year 1990-91, and estimated to be about 230 million tonnes by the year 2000AD. This could be possible due to use of improved agricultural practices, high yield varieties of seeds, irrigation systems land reclamation, mechanisation of farm operations and use of fertilizers and chemicals. The long-term use of inorganic fertilizers alone will have adverse effect on soil unless it is amply supplemented by irrigation system and organic manure to re-condition the soil. Therefore, the use of available organic wastes for gas and manure will help achieving higher foodgrain production targets.

The use of biogas plant spent slurry as manure gives double advantage of biogas plant. The fibrous material, inorganic solids which can't digest or convert into methane, either settle down in the plant or come out with slurry liquid through outlet. This contains many rich and nutritive elements including nitrogen, phosphorous, potassium, iron and trace element (Zn, Fe, Ni, Cu, Cd, Cr, Boron, Calcium, Sodium, etc.)

The Table 1 shows the potential of production of chemical fertilizers and approximate quantity of organic manure required to maintain soil fertility.

Table 1

Capacity, Production and Consumption of NPK in Thousand Tonnes

Year	*Capacity*		*Production*		*Consumption*		*Organic Manure Required*
	N	P_2O_5	*N*	P_2O_5	*N*	P_2O_5	
1951-52	88.8	27.1	28.9	9.8	58.7	6.9	-
1971-72	1487.0	534.4	949.2	290.3	1798.0	2582.0	300
1989-90	8023.0	2453.0	6231.0	2109.0	8570.0	2969.0	1350
1994-95	11590.0	3247.0	9306.0	2556.0	-	-	-
1999-2000	14250.0	4805.0	11400.0	4180.0	-	-	-

The demand of organic manure can be quickly met by recycling of available organic wastes from households, dairy, agro-industries, food processing industries and crop residues. The anaerobic digestion through recycling will not only provide sanitation but gives biogas and enriched manure.

In India, it is estimated that 6.6 and 5.72 million tonnes of NPK would be available to soil, if the cattle and buffalos wastes and human excreta are recycled every year through biogas plants.

The organic wastes have tremendous potential in terms of NPK (Table 2). These organic wastes can be fermented aerobically or in Farm Yard Manure (FYM) pits. The FYM process is slow, takes 4-6 months, creates pollution of environment and results in lose of manure and NPK. The Table 3 shows the comparative properties of FYM and anaerobically digested sludge.

Table 2

Potential of Organic and Biological Resources

Source	Potential (Million tonnes yr)			Nutrients (Million tonnes)		
	Dung	Urine	Biomass	N	P_2O_5	K_2O
Cattle	744.57	480.15	-	0.98	0.79	1.33
Buffalo	258.02	178.75	-	0.75	0.28	0.49
Goat & Sheep	12.23	7.92	-	0.21	0.06	0.02
Pig	4.60	3.99	-	0.04	0.03	0.03
Poultry farm	3.40	-	-	0.03	0.02	0.01
Other livestock	6.2	4.10	-	0.08	0.02	0.07
Human beings	30.38	274.10	-	3.23	0.78	0.72
Crop residues	-	-	100	0.50	0.60	1.50
Forest litter	-	-	15	0.08	0.03	0.08
Water hyacinth compost	-	-	3	0.06	0.03	0.08
Rural compost	-	-	226	1.13	0.63	1.13
Urban compost	-	-	6	0.02	0.02	0.03
Sewage sludge	-	-	0.3	0.01	0.01	0.01
Rhizobium	-	-	24m @ 30-400 kg N/na	1.00	-	-
Non-leaumes	-	-	10m @ 35kg N/ha	0.15	-	-
Blue-green algae	-	-	30m @ 25kg Nha	0.75	-	-

Table 3

Nutrients in FYM and Biogas Slurry

Type of Manure	Time of Mattering	Losses in Quantity	Available		
			N	P	K
1. Farm yard manure composting without cover	4-6 months	45%	0.75	0.6	0.6
2. Farm year manure composted under cover and well cured	3-4 months	20.25%	0.9	0.75	0.75
3. Biogas slurry	1-2 months	07.10%	1.75-2.0	1.0-2.0	1.0-2.0

Method of Handling the Slurry

The biogas plant slurry can be dried or applied directly. The method will mainly depend on the raw material used for fermentation. Accordingly the digested material may consist of two parts:

(i) Liquid - Rich in NPK and micro-nutrient.

(ii) Sludge - Containing NPK, trace element & heavy metals.

Accordingly the following methods are used for handling the slurry:

Wet Slurry/Liquid Effluent Directly Applied to Field

The animal and agricultural wastes based biogas plant effluents, if fully fermented over a period of 6 to 7 weeks, can be directly mixed with irrigation water and applied to crop. The partially fermented material digests slowly and remains in the soil giving residual effects as FYM for about 6-10 months. The entire nutrients in the slurry are available to soil and crop in this case.

The effluents which contains harmful substances, heavy metals and pathogens are not recommended for direct application.

The pumping of slurry, as such, to the agricultural field is not done, however, it can be done after further diluting it with water.

Drying in Manure Pit

The slurry if not required for direct application, can be stored in manure pits, normally made of 1×1×1 to 2×2×1 m size along with dry fodder, crop residues etc. kept for 3-4 months. It is not kept more than 1 m deep in order to avoid handling problem. During this period it dries completely and can be applied to field during ploughing before sowing.

This increases the bulk quantity of organic wastes, slightly lowers the nutrients and NPK. The addition of dry biomass lowers the effect of heavy metals and harmful substances, if present in the slurry.

Pre-Treatment before Application

The slurry from sewage sludge and night soil based biogas plant contains pathogens as such, it has to be pre-treated before application.

The night soil contains pathogens. These are not fully destroyed during digestion, if retention time is kept less and also if digester temperature is lower than 35^{0}C. (Table 4).

Table 4

Pathogens in Night Soil Slurry

Type of Pathogens	***Minimum Retention Time in Days***	***Fatality Percentage (35^0 - 37^{0}C)***
Colitire	21	10^4 number
Schisto-some Ova	07	100
Hookworm Ova	10	100
Ascaris Ova	36	98.8

Therefore, killing Ascaris Ova and Colitire before use of slurry is necessary, for which, the slurry should be treated with ammonia or exposed to open sun at 30-35^{0}C, for 2-3 days, otherwise the pathogens may be present in fruit and vegetable crops and have harmful effect.

The slurry of night soil based biogas plant is stored in a heap or in drying pits, some amount of urea is added to it and kept covered to kill the harmful pathogen. The ammonia produced from the urea destroys the pathogens.

The sewage sludge contains plant nutrients and humus forming effect as such it is treated as a valuable organic manure. However, the sludge contaminant accumulates in it during digestion process such as heavy metals, additives (DDT, detergents, etc.), organic pollutants, etc. in such quantities which prevent its direct use in agricultural, otherwise, these may concentrate in the field and effect its fertility adversely. The Table 5 shows the contents of typical urban sewage sludge:

Table 5

Contaminants in Sewage Sludge

1.	*Heavy Metals:*	
	Lead	300-500 mg/kg
	Cadmium	5-15 mg/kg
	Chrome	100-300 mg/kg
	Copper	500-800 mg/kg
	Nickel	50-150 mg/kg
	Quick silver	Approx. 5 mg/kg
	Zinc	2000-4000 mg/kg
2.	*Ogano-Chlorinate Compounds:*	
	Hexa chorobenzene (HCB PCB) (Sum)	0.01-0.2 mg/kg
	Dioxin and furan (sum)	40-750 mg/kg
	Tetra cholorethyiene	01-50 mg/kg
3.	*Other Organic Contaminants:*	
	Polycyclic Aromatic Hydrocarbons	1-6 mg/kg
	Nonyl Phenol (1-10)	1-1000 mg/kg

Therefore, sludge slurry is applied after tests and ensure that its utilisation keep held free of contaminants deposit or after toxic materials are removed before use. The use of pesticide on sludge applied field build up contaminants in the soil.

The Table 6 gives the limits of heavy metals in air dried soil which can be tolerated in soil provided they don't concentrate and pH of soil is not less than 5.

Table 6

Desirable Limits of Heavy Metals in Soil

Heavy Metal	***Light Soil (mg/kg)***	***Other Soil (mg/kg)***
Lead	100	100.0
Cadmium	1	2.0
Chrome	100	100.0
Copper	60	100.0
Nickel	30	50.0
Quick silver	1	1.5
Zinc	150	300.0

The organo halogen compounds should not exceed 500 mg/kg of dry mass and it is not recommended to apply more than 5 tonnes of dry sludge per ha in a period of 3 years.

Systems for Application

Liquid Slurry

The different type of systems or equipment can be used for application of biogas plant spent slurry.

In case of wet slurry applications, if the terrain has a sufficient gradient, fixed irrigation channels can be used for transport and application of the slurry. It can also be mixed with irrigation water at the point where water enters the main channel or to the field. Care must be taken to flush out deposited slurry in the channel to avoid its blockage.

The process is very convenient and requires little labour only. It can be employed if irrigation schedule for different field is worked out depending on the quantity of slurry available.

Where the irrigation channels are not laid, the transport of slurry in bucket or wheel barrows with tank or other containers fixed over it are used, is then applied to field near crop roots (Figure 1).

Figure 1
Slurry Handling

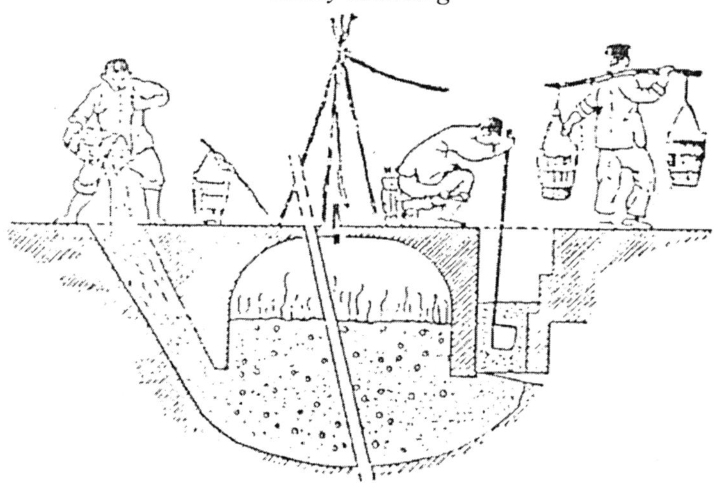

The liquid slurry can be uniformly spread in the field most conveniently before sowing also. It can also be applied during sowing or planting in rows through furrows or seed holes. This gives more advantages in term of gain yield in comparison to dry slurry.

Dry Slurry

The wet slurry if not applied to fields, is stored in manure pit, along with dry organic wastes such as plant leaves, dry fodder, etc, to ferment and dry. The losses of nutrients of slurry can be controlled by drying it in 1 m deep manure pit.

The dry slurry is transported and spread in the field uniformly before ploughing. The slurry mixes well in the soil during ploughing and available to roots uniformly throughout the depth of the field.

However, the transport of liquid material is cumbersome and it becomes difficult for long distance transport. For filling of wheel barrow, scoop with long handles are most convenient and always used. Besides buckets in many cases. The scoops are also useful for uniform spreading of liquid slurry in the field.

Effect of Use of Slurry

The effect of use of biogas slurry has been studied at many places by several scientists and its reported that use of slurry alone or mixed with other chemical fertilizers increases crop yield in comparison to similar treatments with FYM.

It is also reported that quality of fruits or vegetables were superior in comparison to farm yard manure.

The Table 7 and 8 show the results of application of slurry and FYM on yield of different crops.

Table 7

Comparison of Yield from Application of FYM and Slurry

Crop/ Vegetable	*Yield quintal/ha*		*Remarks*
	FYM	*Slurry*	
1. Mustard	54.61	60.41	
2. Gram	8.75	11.03	
3. Berseem	196.66	233.32	
4. Oat	221.66	234.00	
5. MP Chari	30.55	23.97	
6. Cabbage	77.96	96.00	
7. Tomato	187.00	198.00	Good in size & quality
8. Potato	13.6	20.00	-do-

The weed population in slurry plots was much less than FYM plots, therefore, use of biogas plant slurry reduces the cost of labour involved in cleaning the weeds from the field.

The regular analysis of soil was also done to study the residual effect of slurry for six crops in comparison to FYM. It was observed that during first two crops the amount of nutrients available to plant are more in case of slurry than FYM. However, during subsequent years the available nutrients were same in both the cases. This shows that slurry should be applied during each crop and at regular interval.

Table 8

Effect of Different Fertilizer on Yield of Wheat (Mean 4 yrs)

Treatment	***Yield Quintal/ha***	***Percentage Increase***
Control	08.53	-
40 kg N-FYM	10.65	24.85
40 kg N-FYM+20 kg N-Urea	12.87	50.87
40 kg N-FYM+20kg P_2O_5-SP	11.22	31.53
80 kg N-FYM	12.18	42.79
40 kg N-Slurry	13.11	53.69
40 kg N-Slurry+20 kg N-Urea	13.97	63.77
40 kg N-Slurry+20 kg N- P_2O_5-SP	13.30	55.92
80 kg N-Slurry	14.20	66.47
40 kg N-Urea	12.56	47.24
40 kg N-Urea+20 kg P_2O_5-SP	12.88	49.82
20 kg P_2O_5-SP	10.00	17.23
"F" Test	Significant	
"SEm	0.19	
CD at 5%	0.55	

Other Applications of Slurry

The biogas plant slurry has many other applications such as for pscicultre, wormiculture, algae and mushroom production, etc.

(i) *In Pscicultures*: The biogas slurry has been used in fish bond resulting in healthy growth of fish, control of common disease and improving fish quality.

It is proposed that addition of biogas plant slurry increase the level of dissolved oxygen in pond water thus helping in more activities and increase in weight of the fishes.

The slurry does not contain harmful bacteria, pathogens and media for growth of disease prone bacteria as such the level of disease in fishes reduced from 60-70 per cent to 5 per cent.

The slurry helps in quick growth of algae, a food of liking of fishes, and makes available additional nitrogen as such the nutrient contents such as protein, amino acid and lysine increase in the pond fishes. It has been reported that in an experiment, conducted in India and China, the use of slurry increased the quantity of crop and reduced the harvest period. In 0.1 ha of pond area in 11 months time 762 kg of fish was produced with application of biogas slurry. This is a commendable performance without use of artificial feed. Similarly two crops of catla and silver fishes were raised in six months where they grown to 530g and 900g respectively.

(ii) *In Mushroom Production*: The biogas slurry helps in development of excellent media for culture of edible fungi. This improves the quality and yield of mushroom. The growth time was 3-4 days faster and pick up time reduced by 3-7 days with increase in yield by 19-26 per cent. On an average 100 kg rice stalk can harvest 50-100 kg mushroom.

The residues of mushroom and stalk can be used as feed for pig, cattle and other animals as it contains more protein.

Integrated Recycling of Wastes

The Figure 2 shows the integrated recycling of organic wastes to get food, fodder and fuel.

Figure 2

Integrated Recycling of Organic Wastes

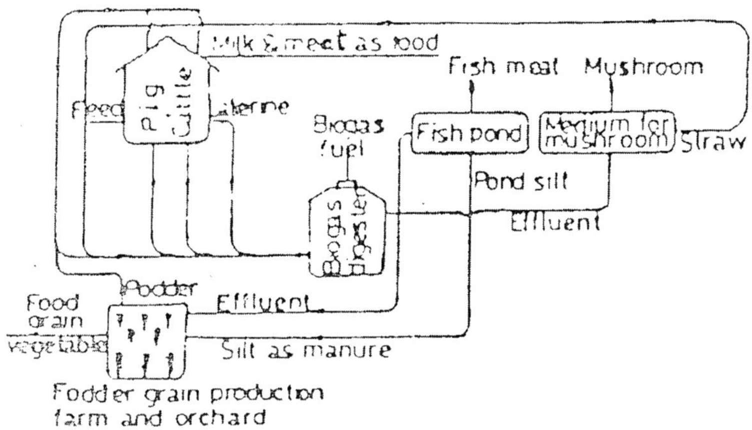

Conclusion

The digested slurry, an effluent of biogas plant has good nutritive value and should be utilised for increasing crop production and soil fertility. Presently, various methods of handling and utilisation of digested slurry are available. It is essential to maximise the use of nutrients available in the digested slurry for crop production at appropriate time.

Chapter 6

Role of FYM in Improving Fertility and Crop Response

Dr. B.L. Gaur
Professor, Agronomy, RCA, Udaipur

Farmyard Manure (FYM)

The term Farmyard Manure refer to the decomposed mixture of dung and urine of farm animals along with the litter (bedding material and left over material from roughages or fodder fed to cattle). Farmyard manure collected daily from the cattleshed consists mainly of dung and part of the urine soaked in refuse, newly collected and stored FYM is fresh as against well decomposed FYM which has been stored for a sufficient period of time to allow its decomposition to completion. On an average well decomposed FYM contains 0.5 per cent N, 0.2 per cent P_2O_5 and 0.5 per cent K_2O (Yawalkar *et al.*, 1977).

Role of FYM

Improvement in Soil Fertility and Plant Growth

Since farmyard manure contain major and minor plant nutrients, it has direct effect on soil fertility and plant growth.

Improvement in Physical Condition of Soil

FYM application increases organic matter content of soil hence improve the physical properties of soils. This effect is very important in case of most of our arable lands. FYM increases the humes content of the soil and consequently the water holding capacity of light soils is increased and the drainage of heavy soils is improved.

Providing Food Soil Organisms

FYM act as food material for soil micro-organisms, thereby increases the activity of microbes which, in turn, helps in converting unavailable plant nutrients into available form.

Regulation of Soil Temperature

Application of FYM also acts as mulching material and thus helps in keeping soil temperature down and improving soil air movement under condition of drought.

Maintenance of Soil Fertility

Prolong use of FYM maintains as well as builds the fertility of the soil and does not impoverish the soil, as happens due to offensive use of chemical fertilizers. It does not mortgage the farmers future to the availability of high cost chemical fertilizers.

Nutrients Supply by FYM

On an average well decomposed FYM applied to various crops by the cultivators, contains the following major plant nutrients beside minor elements.

Nitrogen - 0.5%, Phosphorus - 0.2%. Based on the per cent nutrient contents, an average dressing of 10 tons of FYM per hectare supplies about 50 kg N, 20 kg P_2O_5 and 50 kg K_2O/ha. However, all of these quantities are not available to crop in the year of application, particularly nitrogen which is very slow acting. Only one-third of the nitrogen is likely to be used by the crop in the first year. About two-third of the phosphorus may be used and most of the potash will be available during first year. This effect of FYM application on the yield of first crop is known as the direct effect of application.

The remaining amount of plant food becomes available to second, third and to a small extent to the fourth crop raised on the same piece of land. This phenomenon is known as the residual effect of FYM. When the FYM is applied ever year, the crop yield goes on increasing due to direct plus residual effect on every succeeding crop. This beneficial effect is also known as cumulative effect.

Crop Response to FYM

Results of the experiments conducted during last several years and the experience of cultivators have indicated that most the field crops responds to FYM application, though certain crops are more responsive to FYM while certain crops are less responsive.

Crops which show profitable response to application of FYM are vegetable crops, specially potatoes, tomatoes, sweet potato, water melons, radish, carrot, cauliflower, turnip, onion, garlic etc., sugarcane, rice, jute, and fruit trees like oranges, bananas, grapes, apples, guavas, mangoes etc.

The crop show moderate response to application of FYM are cereals like Jowar, Maize, Bajara, Wheat, Ragi, Barley, Oats, oil seed crops like groundnut, linseed, sesame, castor, coconut and cash crops like cotton. Positive response to FYM application and its beneficial effect on crop yields have been reported by workers like Grewal *et al.* (1984), Ponsica *et al.* (1986), and Gaur (1992) in maize; Devasenapathy and Subbarao (1985) in sorghum; Khan *et al.* (1986), Rajput and Warsi (1991) and Sharma and Mitra (1991) in rice; Mishra *et al.* (1969) in sugarcane; Chawle *et al.* (1993) and Balsubramanian and Palaniappan (1994) in groundnut; Sarkar *et al.* (1997) in pigeanpea; Singh and Singh (1997) in sunflower; Singh *et al.* (1997) in potato, Tiwari *et al.* (1995) and Badiyala and Verma (1991) in maize + soybean-wheat cropping system.

Field Management of FYM

The quantity and quality of FYM and its method and time of application has a great relevance with crop yield is not known by the farmers. Most of the farmers apply sub-optimal dose of FYM to crop fields at their own convenient time and method which is not scientific. Under field conditions, most of the cultivators unload FYM in small piles in the field before applying. The manure is left in piles for a month or more before it is applied. Also the FYM is often ploughed in or disced a few days after spreading, both the practices are faulty. Plant nutrients are lost through heating and drying when the manure is left in small piles during the summer months. This leads to reduced efficiency of manure (Table 1).

Table 1

Relative Effectiveness of FYM in Increasing Crop Yield when Ploughed under Immediately or Left in Piles in the Field

Treatment	***Relative Value in Increasing Crop Yield (%)***
1. Manure spread and mixed with the soil immediately	100
2. Manure kept in piles for 2 days before spreading	80
3. Manure kept in piles for 14 days before spreading	55

FYM that is spread on surface but not mixed with soil for several days, looses its potentiality for increasing crop yields much more than that of manure left in piles for several days but spread and mixed with soil immediately. Major loss through quick heating and drying of FYM is of element, nitrogen. N escapes as an elemental gas by volatilisation (Table 2).

Table 2

Relative Effectiveness of FYM in Increasing Crop Yield when Mixed with Soil at Different Times after Spreading

Treatment	***Relative Value (%)***
1. Manure ploughed under immediately	100
2. Manure ploughed under 6 hours after spreading	86
3. Manure ploughed under 24 hours after spreading	70
4. Manure ploughed under 36 hours after spreading	44

Source: Yawalkar *et al.*, 1977.

Thus to derive maximum benefit from FYM, it is essential that it should be spread evenly and mix with soil immediately. Further, to increase the availability of plant nutrients by FYM in first year crop, it is advisable to apply recommended dose of FYM, 3-4 weeks before sowing of the crop.

References

Badiyala, D. and Verma, S.P., 1991. "Integrated nitrogen management in maize + soybean - wheat cropping sequence." *Indian J. Agron.* 36(4): 497-501.

Balasubramanian, P. and Palaniappan, S., 1994. "Effect of combined application of bacterial inoculation along with FYM on irrigated groundnut." *Indian J. Agron.* 39(1): 131-133.

Chawle, V.V., Bharad, G.M., Kohale, S.K. and Nagdev, M.B., 1993. "Effect of N and FYM levels on growth and yield of summer groundnut." *Indian J. Agron.* 38(3): 500-502.

Devasenapathy, P. and Subbaraw, M., 1985. "Effect of N, FYM, and iron on sorghum," *Madras Agric. J.* 2(11): 622-625.

Gaur, B.L., 1989. "Effect of time of application and N rates on the yield of rainfed maize." *Indian. J. Agron.* 36(1): 107-108.

Grewal, S.S., Sud, A.D., Mittal, S.P. and Singh, K., 1984. "Effect of FYM and chemical fertilizer on yield of rainfed maize in Siwalik foot." *Indian J. Agron.* 27(3): 282-283.

Khan, S.K., Mohanti, S.K. and Chalam, P., 1986. "Integrated management of organic manure and fertilizer nitrogen for rice." *J. Indian Soc. Soil Sci.* 34(2): 505-509.

Mishra, G.N., Mukerji, B.K. and Verma, G., 1969. "Comparative response of sugarcane to organic and inorganic manure applied singly and in combination. Manuring of sugarcane." *Agric. Review Proc. 19th Annual Con. Sug. Tech. Assoc. India*, Pt, I. 46-49.

Ponosica, E.P., Escalada, R.G. and Quirol, B.F., 1986. "Effect of FYM application on the growth and yield of corn." *Field Crop Abstr.* 89(6): 4136.

Rajput, A.L. and Warsi, A.S., 1991. "Contribution of organic materials to nitrogen economy in rice production." *Indian J. Agron.* 36(3): 455-456.

Sarkar, R.K., Shit, D. and Chakraborty, A., 1997. "Effect of levels and sources of phosphorus with and without FYM on pigeonpea." *Indian J. Agron.* 42(1): 120-123.

Sharma. A.R. and Mitra, B.N., 1991. "Direct and residual effect of organic materials in rice based cropping system." *Indian J. Agron.* 36(3): 299-303.

Singh, J. and Singh, K.P. 1997. "Integrated nutrient management in sunflower," *Indian J. Agron*, 42(2): 370-374.

Singh, S.P., Singh, V. and Lakhan, R., 1996. "Effect of phosphorus and FYM application on yield of potato." *Indian J. Agron.* 41(4): 630-632.

Tiwari, K.P., Namdeo, K.N., Tomar, P.K.S. and Raghu, J.S., 1995. "Effect of macro and micro nutrients in combination with organic manures on the production of sesame." *Indian J. Agron.* 40(1): 134-136.

Yawalkar, K.S., Agrawal, J.P. and Bokde, S., 1977. *Manures and Fertilizers*. 4th Ed. Agri. Horticultural Publishing House, Nagpur. India.

Chapter 7

Recycling of Lignocellulolytic Farm Waste through Vermicomposting

M.S. Acharya
In-charge, KVK, Jhalawar, Rajasthan

Introduction

Organic farming has an important place in agriculture to sustain the productivity of soil for a long period. Use of chemical fertilizers, high yielding varieties and better irrigation facilities have helped in attaining the self sufficiency in food production, however the use of chemical fertilizer varies. Moreover, the further increase in fertilizer input to 25 million tons of nutrients to achieve 200 m ton of foodgrain (ratio 1:8) is restricted due to limited sources of fossil fuel and raw materials. In India, organic manures contribute only 4 million tons of nutrients, although there exists a potential source of 13 million tons if the estimated amount of organic waste is recycled (Vimal and Talashilkar, 1983). Since it is not possible to recycle all the available wastes, part of it can be diverted to supplement the increasing demand of nutrients and earthworms can help in improving the recycling process. It would also help in keeping the environment eco-friendly. Compost prepared from lignocellulolytic wastes and cowdung using earthworms containing castings, faeces, earthworms, cocoon, micro-organism nutrients etc. is known as vermicompost.

Advantages of Vermicompost (Shroff and Devasthali, 1992)

1. Vermicompost is a source of soil carbon and humus and activates soil micro-organism involved in transformations of nutrients. It also improves soil structure, drainage, aeration, water holding capacity, action exchange capacity etc.
2. It provides balanced nutrition to crops giving good yields and better quality of produce.
3. It helps in reducing the number of irrigations and quantity of water for each irrigation.
4. It provides resistance to plants against plant pathogens and insects thereby reduces the requirements of agrochemicals.
5. It helps in reducing the pollution of soil, water and food products by recycling of farm waste and reduced uses of chemical fertilizers.

Compared to farmyard manure, vermicompost in rich in nitrogen, phosphorus and potassium. It is also a good source of nutrients like zinc, copper, calcium, magnesium, sulphur, cobalt etc.

Earthworms for Composting

India has about 3,000 species of earthworms which are adapted to a range of environment and vermiculture heeds. Earthworms can be divided into the following two broad categories:

I. Epigeic the surface living worm
II. Epianecic - the burrowing worms

Epigeic or manure worms are found on the surface and are reddish brown in colour. They do not process the soil but are efficient in composting of organic wastes and enhance the bio-degradation. When maintained in captivity under semi-natural conditions, they remain active throughout the year.

Epianecic species burrow and mix the soil from different horizons in the profile. They ingest organic and soil fractions and bring organo-mineral crumbs to surface.

Reproduction of Earthworms

The reproduction of earthworms depends on temperature, moisture and availability of food materials. Under optimum condition, earthworms become adults in 4 weeks and reproduce. One adult gives 2-3 cocoon in a week till the density of worms restricts the rate of reproduction. Optimum temperature range is 25-30^{0}C and moisture is about 30 per cent.

Comparative Production of Conventional Compost and Vermicompost

Pit of 120 cu.ft. gives about one ton of compost per year by conventional method, whereas 6-7 tons of compost is produced when it is mediated by earthworm.

Preparation of Compost

Vermicomposting requires temperature in the range of 25-30^{0}C, optimum moisture and dark conditions. Temperature can be maintained by providing shadow with trees, sheds etc. It checks direct sunlight specially in summer periods. Moisture can be maintained by sprinkling water as and when required specially during summers and protecting the beds from rains to have excess water. Dark conditions are maintained by covering beds with gunny bags, tripal, etc.

Vermicomposting in Shallow Beds

Prepare a bed of 40-50' length, 3' width and 1' depth and cover it with shed of 4-4.5' height to protect the bed from direct sunlight and rain ((Fig. 1).

Figure 1

Layering of Compost Bed

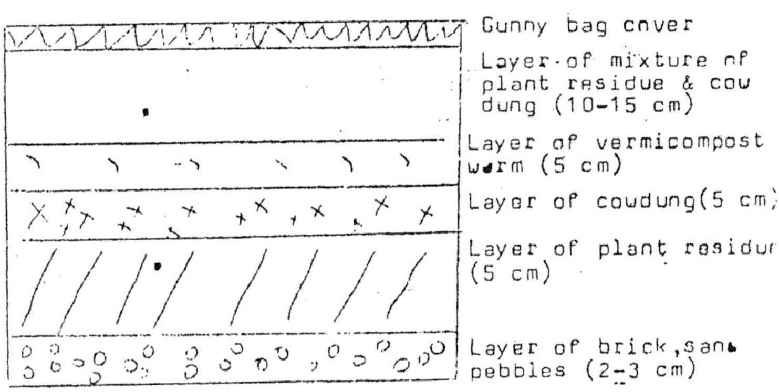

At the bottom, provide a 2-3 cm thick layer of broken brick pieces, pebbles, sand etc. This layer is inhabited by earthworms. Over this layer, prepare a 50 cm thick layer with residues of sorghum, maize, sugarcane etc., followed by a 50 cm thick layer of partially degraded cowdung. Moist the layer by sprinkling water. Cowdung layer is over layered by a 5.0 cm thick layer from vermicompost containing cocoons and adult worms. This layer is also moistened by sprinkling water. Vermicompost layer is followed by 10-15 cm thick layer of mixture of grasses, leaves, crop residues, and dung. Cover the pit with gunny bags and sprinkle water regularly as required to maintain the moisture (about 30%).

Earthworms start ingesting decaying lignocellulolytic materials and leaves, branches, roots and other. Plant residues are converted into compost in about 2 months period. Worms leave their casting over the surface till composting is completed and they come to the surface. Change of colour of mixture to black and presence of worms on surface indicate that compost is ready. Bed of 40×3×1 cu.ft. gives about 1 ton of compost in first two months. Subsequently one can harvest one ton of compost every months.

Vermicomposting in Pit

Prepare a pit of 180 cm length, 90cm width and 90cm height at elevated place and under shadow of trees etc. At the bottom prepare a layer (15-10 cm thick) of brick pieces, pebbles and sand keeping raised from the centres. Over this prepare a layer of organic residues (5.0 cm) followed by 5.0 cm thick layer of partially decomposed cowdung or compost. This layer is over layered by a 5.0 cm thick layer of vermicompost containing a live earthworms - 200-300, and cocoons. After about four weeks, another layer of 5.0 cm thick from the mixture cowdung, leaves, grasses etc. Is prepared and moist the layers. This layer is repeated every 4-5 days till the pit is filled completely always as and when required. When the compost is ready stop watering to dry the surface layers so that worms migrate to deeper layers and harvest surface layers. Since and use the compost. One pit gives about 1 ton of compost every month (Fig. 2).

Figure 2
Layering of Compost Pit

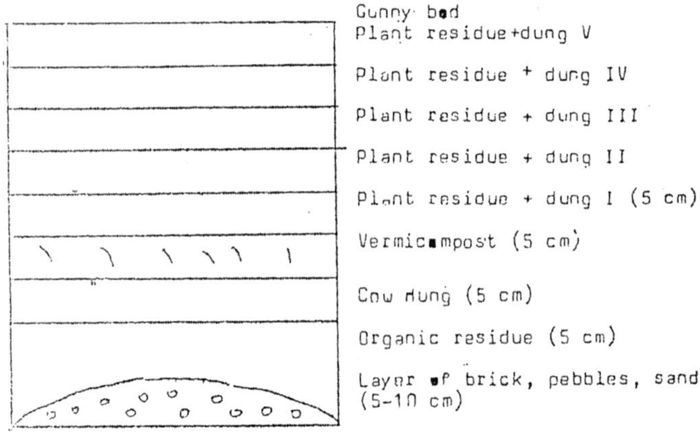

Vermicomposting in Box

Composting in box is done where it is required in small scale for kitchen garden etc. Take a box of about 60 cm×50cm×50cm. At the bottom put a layer of 5 cm thick from stone degrading residues of corm, sorghum, sugarcane etc. Followed by 5-8 cm thick layer of cowdung. Over the cowdung put a thin layer of fresh vermicompost containing a live adult earthworms - 200 nos. This layer is over layered by 15-20 cm thick layer of mixture containing cowdung, kitchen wastes, garden waste etc. Cover the surface with jute cloth and moist from time to time to maintain a moisture of about 30 per cent. Protect the box from hot and cold weather. Compost will be ready in 30-45 days and harvest by drying surface layers (Fig. 3).

Figure 3
Layering in Box

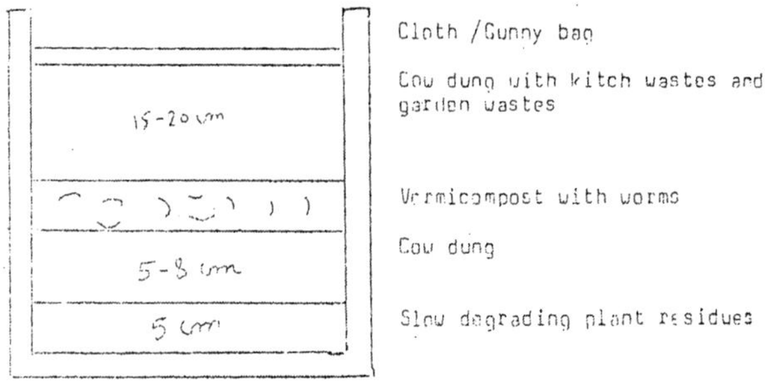

References

Shroff, V.N. and Devasthali, S. 1992. In: *Proc. Nat. Sem. Natural Farming* (Ed.) L.L. Somani, K.L Totawat & B.L Baser, Rajasthan College of Agri., Udaipur.

Vimal, O.P. and Talashilkar, S. 1983. *J. Sci. Ind. Res.* 42:115.

Chapter 8

Compost: A Method of Recycling Plant Nutrients

B.N. Swami
Dept. of Agri. Chem. & Soil Science, RCA, Udaipur

"Rich in manure, rich in fruit"

—*Atharva Veda Samhita*, Circa 350 BC

"No fodder, no cattle; no cattle, no manure; no manure, no crop"

—Ancient Tamil Proverb

Introduction

Nutrient deficiency is the major limiting factor for crop production in most of the world soils and phenomenal increase in production obtained in the last two decades are attributable to a greater extent to the removal of this constraint through use of fertilizers. For example, in India based on the calculation of National Commission on Agriculture, India (1976) as well as Kanwar (1982), 130 million tonnes of foodgrain produced in 1980-81 removed 18 million tonnes of nutrients. The amount of N, P, K added through fertilizer during 1980-81 was only 5.5 million tonnes. An additional 5 million tonnes of nutrients could be replenished through organic manure resources. This will leaves 7.5 million tonnes of nutrients which were drained of P from the soil. In addition to this, India is loosing 8.4 million tonnes of NPK through erosion. Other nutrients are similarly depleted. Can the soil bank remain solvent with this type of balance sheet?

While the use of mineral fertilizers is quickest and surest way of boosting crop production, their cost and other constraints frequently deters farmers from using them in recommended quantities and in balanced proportions. As a consequence of this and other constraints there seems to be no option but to fully exploit potential alternative sources of plant nutrients. Complementary use of available renewable sources of plant nutrients (organic/biological) along with mineral fertilizers is of great importance for the maintenance of soil productivity.

Organic manures have been time tested materials for improving the productivity of the soils. It is, however only during the last 10-15 years that these have been incorporated into integrated nutrient supply system for intensive high yielding cropping sequences in contrast to the subsistence level in the production of the past. Of the organic manures used by farmers under Indian conditions, farmyard manure and compost rank as the two most important ones that deserve attention. This is confined to compost, other related material, will be covered by other speakers of this training programme.

Historical Background

The act of collecting and utilising all available wastes, from human, animal and vegetable sources, and converting them into manure was known to the Indian, Japanese and Chinese farmers from very ancient times. Scientific interest in this subject started since Richards and Hutchinson (1921) in England converted straw to "artificial humus" or synthetic manure. This work also led to the systematic preparation of composts for rural and urban wastes in larger area in all parts of the world. In the method advocated by Richards and Hutchinson use was made of a starter in the form of powder called 'Adco' (from Agricultural Development Company). Fowler (1927) gave out a technique called activated composting method. It was called adivated since a suitably prepared inoculum was used to introduce the necessary micro-organisms for decomposing the material. Howard and Wad (1931) worked out the process of composting at Indore between 1924 and 1931. The method is essentially aerobic and decomposition is affected in shallow pits with occasion turnings. Acharya and Subrahamanyan (1939) developed Bangalore hot fermentation method, rather simply 'Banglaore' method, essentially an anaerobic method because they observed heavy losses of nitrogen in all aerobic methods. Acharya (1940) observed superiority of Bangalore hot fermentation method over aerobic shallow trench method and aerobic heap method with respect to yield of manure and conservation of nitrogen.

What is Compost?

Composing differs from other decomposing systems in that temperature and rate of decomposition are usually altered by positive human intervention. The world compost literally means a substitute for a natural product and originally compost was a term used by Richards and Hutchinson (1921) for artificial humus or synthetic manure. They used these terms for the artificial product produced by them since it looked very much alike to farm yard manure. Somani (1998) compiled various definitions description of compost. The shorter Oxford dictionary defined composting is the process of making into a mixed manure of organic nature. Biddlestone and Gray defines composting as the decomposition of heterogeneous organic matter by a mixed microbial population in a most warm aerobic environment. Bell and Bose defines it as an aerobic thermophillic decomposition process while miller states that in its broadest sense composting may be defined as in complete microbial degradation of organic waste, where the microbial process may vary from aerobic to anaerobic and may lead more or less extensive degradation.

Compost are broadly divided into two groups such a rural compost or farm compost and town or urban compost. Although the essential principles underlying the preparation are the same, the two differ in regard to the composting materials used and in the composition of the final product obtained. On a percentage dry weight basis the compost will contain 0.4 to 3.5 per cent nitrogen (as N), 0.3 to 3.5 per cent phosphorus (as P_2O_5) and 0.5 to 2.0 per cent Potassium (as K_2O). Besides the three manurial ingredients, it also contains calcium and magnesium and is a valuable carrier of practically all minor elements. Some of these like iron are in a form readily available to plants. Further, the reducing action and chelating effect that the soluble organic matter produces in the soil help to keep phosphorus, iron and manganese in a mobile form. Important factors which need to be maintained at optimum level for efficient composting are C:N ratio, C:P ratio, particle size, blending or proportions of raw materials moisture, aeration, temperature distruction of pathogens and parasites and use of microbial activators. Gaur (1992) summarised parameters which need to be maintained its optimum level for efficient composting (Table 1).

Table 1

Optimum Values Composting Parameters

Parameter	***Optimum Value for Composting***
C:N ratio of feed	25 to 35
Particle size	10 mm for agitated systems and forced aeration, 50 mm for long heaps and natural aeration.
Moisture content	50 to 60 per cent (higher values possible when using bulking agents)
Air flow	0.6 to 1.8 m^3 air/day/kg volatile solids during thermophillic stage, or maintain oxygen level at 10 to 18 percent
Temperature	55 to 60^0C held for 3 days
Agitation	No agitation to periodic turning in simple systems and short bursts of vigorous agitation in mechanised systems
pH control	Normally not necessary
Heap size	Any length, 1.5 m high and 2.5 m wide for heaps using natural aeration. With forced aeration, heap size depends on need to avoid overheating
Activators	Use of efficient cellulolytic fungi and bio-fertilizers

Source: Gaur, 1992.

Advantages of Composting as an Agricultural Wastes Disposal Method

Somani (1998) tested following advantages of composting as an agricultural waste disposal method:

1. It reduces the bulk volume of the waste.
2. It yields a stable product.

3. It leads to the distruction of pathogenic bacteria and of the eggs of para sites.
4. It allows organic wastes to be recycled without distruction of their in net high energy value.
5. It reduces risk polluting water courses.
6. It helps to conserve increasingly expensive fertilizers.

Beneficial Effects of Compost in Crop Production

The beneficial effects by the use of organic manure in crop production are many. But its chief value; depends on the amounts of nutrients, particularly nitrogen, it can supply to growing crop. Gaur (1992) discussed in detail the beneficial effects of compost on soil properties and crop production. Voluminous literature is available on beneficial effect of manure of compost on soil properties and productivity.

Soil Properties

Physical Effects

1. It improves soil physical conditions like structure, texture and tilth, etc.
2. It increases water holding capacity of the soils which provide protection to the crops against drought.
3. It helps in control of soils erosion.

Chemical Effects

1. It improves phosphorus availability.
2. It increases efficiency of fertilizer nutrients.
3. It helps in partial replacement of fertilizers which involve greater energy/expense.

Biological Effects

1. It increases population of beneficial soil micro-organising like, actinonycetes and fungi which help in production of polysaccharides and in building better soil structure.
2. It increases N fixation and P solubilisation due to increase in the population of.

Crop Yields

Numerous experiments have been conducted to study the response of crops to compost. The magnitude of response depends upon on the type of manure and its quality, time of application, doses per unit area, soil characteristics and moisture required during the crop growth season (Gaur, 1992). A summary of yield responses to 12.6 FYM or compost/ha was given by Gaur *et al.* in 1990 (Table 2).

Table 2

Response of Different Crops to Compost/Farmyard Manure

Crop	*Number of Stations*	*Number of Experi-ments*	*Unit*	*Response Kg/ha to 12.6 t/ha Manure**		
				Mini-mum	*Maxi-mum*	*Average*
Rice	63	34	Kg paddy/ha	100	216	168
Wheat (irrigated)	31	210	Kg grain/ha	82	296	202
Wheat (unirrigated)	14	71	Kg grain/ha	74	140	85
Sugarcane*	19	258	T cane/ha	3.7	11.7	80
Cotton (irrigated)	10	71	Kg lint/ha	48.9	96.1	56.4
Cotton (unirrigated)	25	294	Kg lint/ha	11.8	22.3	16.2

* FYM to sugarcane added at 25 t/ha.

Source: Gaur *et al.*, 1990.

Long-Term Effects

Long-term manurial experiments conducted in India during 1980-85 showed a decline trend in productivity with application of N, P, and K alone (Nambiar & Abrol, 1989). The superiority of integrated use of organic; manures and chemical fertilizers in sustaining crop productivity in intensive farming systems in comparison to chemical fertilizers alone has been observed by number of workers (Lal *et al.*, 1986; Mambier & Abrol, 1989).

Essentials of Composting

Basic requirements for compost making are the compostable waste material, air, moisture and a small amount of soluble nitrogen. The micro-organisms require so little quantity of phosphorus and potassium that the decomposing materials already contain enough of them and no outside addition is proposed to be necessary.

Process of Composting

Composting is largely a biological process in which micro-organisms of both types, namely aerobic (which require air or oxygen gas for development) and an aerobic (which functions in absence of air or oxygen) decompose organic matter under medium to high temperatures and lower the carbon-nitrogen ratio of the refuse (Yawalkar *et al.*, 1996). Normally, composting process's completed in 3-6 months yielding an amorphous brown to dark brown humified material called humus is produced. The microbial activities during composting of four phases namely mesophillic, thermopillic, cooling and maturing. There is no precise shape and magnitude of temperature vs time curve because it is influenced by number of factors. In a typical composting, pH of the mass of initially slightly acid during the mesophillic stage of composting. In the thermophillic stage the pH rises rapidly to 8.0 to 9.0 as ammonia is evolved. During the cooling stage, the pH falls towards neutrality of composting is to proceed rapidly an adequate supply to the madella of the mass of composting material must be maintained. The supply of oxygen can be increased by blowing air into the compost, agitation, the provision of air vents into the base of the composting mass or by turning. If however, the rate of air flow through compost is too great, heat losses and desiccation will occur and the rate of composting will be reduced.

Particle size and interparticle void size both influence the process of composting. When particle size is small, rate of microbial decomposition is enhanced. If particle size too small, the inter particle voids are reduced in size and rate oxygen and carbon dioxide diffusion will be reduced. Small particle size will also improve the insulating properties of the compost thus retaining heat within the compost.

Nitrogen is the major nutrient required by the M.O in the assimilation of the carbon substracts in organic wastes. The overall loss of the nitrogen from nitrogen rich system may be accompanied by an increase in the protein content of the compost. Once the more readily degradable components have been utilised the major carbon sources rending the compost are cellulose and lignin. Various attempts have been made to describe the decomposition process mathematically.

Changes in Making Compost

The rate of decomposition of various components of organic matter is not same. Normally lignin, fats and waxes decompose very slowly. A good discussion on the decomposition of various components of organic matter is given by Singh (1970).

Methods of Composting

In India, earlier workers have done commendable work on methods of composting. Howard and Wad (1931) worked out a procedure of composting at Indore between 1924 and 1931. The method was recognised throughout the world and became extremely popular by the name of "Indore Method". Farm litter and town waste (Katchra) can be used as a composting material. Procedures have been developed for composting from certain crop residues like from sugar can trash. However, composting is done basically by two composting processes in India namely Indore Method and Bangalore hot fermentation method.

Indore Method

In this method, composting can be done in pits/trenches or heaps. Normally, pits are preferred over heap as quality of compost is decreased in later. In addition to this two or three turnings are required till the compost is ready. It may not be possible to get time and helpers for the extra work at proper time. Heap method is usually followed in the rainy season be cause pits/trenches are likely to be influenced by the water.

Pit/Trench Method

Details are as follows:

1. Pits, each 183 cm wide, 91 cm deep and 915 cm long (or any convenient length) is dug in a very high lying area

where there is less chances of percolation of water or over-flow from the adjoining water channels.

2. All farm wastes are collected for composting woody and hard residues (R) are chopped previously in small pieces and crushed by placing them on farm roads for being trampled over by bullock carts/tractor. Hard material should not exceed 10 per cent of total composting material.
3. The mixed material is spread on the floor of cattle shed as bedding.
4. The urine and dung soaked bedding is removed together with one fourth of entire quantity of dung produced and spread daily in the layers of 2 to 3 inches high in the pit. The layer of waste material is covered with a thin layer of dung and urine earth.
5. This daily charge is watered and continuously dumped in the pit will the entire pit; is covered the surface or is slightly above the takes about 6 days.
6. The first turning of material is done after 16 days charging, second turning after 30 days of charging and third after 60 days of charging. The process needs six watering and three turnings and manure is ready for removal to fields in about 90 days after the initial charging.

Heap Method

This method is also known as rain water compost method and brief details are as follows:

1. The compost heap should be 180-240 cm wide, 107 to 122 cm deep and of a convenient length according to material available for composting.
2. Two turnings are all that needed. In the first being material is thoroughly mixed heap is reduced to half or its original size. Second turning is done in the same manner.
3. The manure is ready for application within a period of three months
4. In localities with heavy rainfall, this method of composting should be followed under a shed to avoid to heavy wasting of nutrients.

Bangalore Method

In Indore method, there are heavy losses of nitrogen as composting process is done under aerobic conditions. Losses of nitrogen can be markedly reduced or even entirely eliminated, if decomposition is done under reduced air supply. Bangalore method is essentially an aerobic and also called as hot fermentation method. The material is allowed to decompose under optimum conditions of moisture and supply for a limited period of 5-6 days in above ground heaps. The temperature begins to fall the supply of air is by putting the decomposing material in an underground trench or pit and sealing off the top with mud plaster. Superiority of Bangalore method over Indore method has been recorded by Acharya, (1940) and Gildayal (1953). This is because of better quality with respect to the nutrients and reduction in water requirement. However, composting period is longer in Bangalore method as compared to Indore method.

Composting of Farm Wastes

In this method, method of filling composting material in the pit is same as described in Indore methods. After filling of pit, composting material is plastered with the clayed soil in order to check losses similar. Compost by this method is ready within six to eight months.

Composting Town Waste

The urban population of India stands about 125 million, urban waste increases with the increase in the population. The urban refuse can be converted into good quality manure by adopting the Bangalore process of composting. The Bangalore method of composting town waste is as follows.

1. In this process, town waste is used which is consisting of night soil, sewage, sludge, street and dust bean refuse, factory waste, wool and cotton etc.
2. The site of composting should be at least 400 m away from the outskirts of the town and should preferably be not situated in the western side of the town since the used generally air flows from west for most part of the year.
3. Composting in this process is carried out in bricklined or kucha trenches. The trenches are so arranged in rows that

the longer sides are parallel in the shorter ends are in same line, leaving 152-213 cm space vacant between successive trenches.

4. Size of the trenches depends upon the population of town and availability of the raw materials. The dimension recommended are as follows:
5. First, a layer of katchra (street sweeping or refuse) about 15 cm thick is spread on the bottom of the trench, with long handled rakes, over this, is added night soil to a thickness of 5 cm. Normally, night soil flow by itself and doesn't require spreading, but its corse it is hard, it may be handled with long handled spade. This the layers of katchra and night soil are added alternatively.
6. At the end of each day, heap is covered with katchra to a thickness 22 cm. If loose earth is available it would be good to the cover top of the heap at the end of each day (weather trench is fall full or completely full) with a layer about 5 cm thick. This thick layer effectively check foul small, conserve moisture better avoids nitrogen losses of minimise the nuisances of files.
7. Each trench after it is filled to the ground level is covered with katchra and earth, so that it rises 30 cm above ground level.
8. In rainy season, it would be advisable to make the top of each heap dome shaped, so that water does not collect in the trenches but flow out.

Table 3

Requirement of Trench Side as Population of Town/City

S. No.	***Population***	***Size of the trench (in cm)***		
		Length	***Width***	***Depth***
1.	Below 5000	475	152	76
2.	5000-10,000	610	183	91
3.	10,000-20,000	762	183	91
4.	20,000-50,000	915	213	91
5.	Above 50,000	915	244	107

Management Aspects

Compost can be applied to all crops and all types of soil but the rates application will very accordingly to soil, crop climate, local availability and also quality of manure.

Rates of Application

The amount of compost to be applied to soil will be determined by:

1. Amount of nutrients, particularly nitrogen, which can be efficiently utilised by the crops,
2. The amount which will not reduce seed fermentation and growth rate of young plants.
3. Amount which can be conveniently incorporated in the soil.

About 25 tonnes/ha is recommended under intensive irrigated cropping conditions for sugarcane, vegetables, potatoes etc. and rice 12.5 tonnes/ha for irrigated or rainfed crops where potential rainfall as medium to heavy (about 125 cm) and 5-7 tonnes/ha in dry areas where mean annual rainfall is about 50 cm. In dry farming areas, application of 2.5 tonnes/ha can give sufficient increase In crop yield.

Time & Method of Application

To derive maximum benefit, the compost should be applied during land preparation and incorporated into soil having adequate moisture about two or three weeks before sowing so that nutrients are made available to the plants. The manure should be ploughed or harrowed into the soil soon after it has been carted to the field and spread over land. An additional application can be made at the time of sowing when it is used in conjunction with mineral fertilizers in ferrous. It is advisable to use compost with a phosphatic fertilizer as to prepare rock phosphate enriched compost (Mishra 1992).

Technologies for Quicker and Better Compost Production

In recent years, workers made efforts of upgrade nutrient content of composts and hasten the composting process so that materialism of better quality can be balanced in less time. These major developments are briefly summarised below:

Compost Accelerator/Inoculants

Processes of isolation and screening cellulose and lignin efficient mocro-organisms are being continuously attempted in the different centres of All India under the ICAR coordinated project on the various aspects of microbiological decompostition and recycling of farm and city wastes. Of the several organisms isolated by different centres *Trichoderma virida* (I 189), Triviride (I 191), *Aspergillus terrens* (I 171), *Aspergellus* spp, *stachybatritys* sp. *Pencicillium* sp. possessed good cellulolytic activity. One species each aspergillus combined ligno lylic activity as well. Two isolates *viz. Pestalotiopsis* versicolar and *Aspergillue* sp. (No 110) possessed strong, lignolytic activity.

Three promising cultures viz. *Trichurus spiralis, staphylotonchem coccosporun and penincellium digite,* lun, significantly hastened the composting of paddy straw in compost pits.

Reinforcement of Compost

Nature usually, compost is badly unbalanced due to presence of five times more readily available nitrogen than active P_2O_5. In order to increase the efficiency of compost, some phosphatic fertilizer is mixed with compost before it is applied to the land. This practice is spoken as reinforcement and compost mixed with super phosphate is also called super compost. Super phosphate is used to reinforce compost for three primary purposes:

1. To reduce losses of nitrogen as ammonia.
2. To increase the percentage of phosphorus in compost to make it a better balanced fertilizer.
3. To increase the efficiency of phosphorus utilisation in the soils that tends to tie up phosphorus.

The super compost can be prepared by applying 1 kg of super phosphate per day in the drain behind each cow. If this is not done, 25 kg super phosphate/tone of compost can be added after manure is in a hydrated lime, ground lime stone and borax may be added in compost to reduce odours to control files.

Enrichment of Compost by Bio-inoculants

Nutrient content of final product of compost can be improved by enrichment of compost with efficient microbial inoculants. Inoculation with Azotobacter and phosphate solubilising culture in presence of 1 per cent rock phosphate is a beneficial input to obtain a good quality compost which is rich in N and available P_2O_5 (Gaur, 1992). The quality of compost produced from dairy farm waste was improved by its inoculation with *Azotobacter* and *Aspergillus* awamon (Tiwari *et al.*, 1989). The effect of this technology was also tested in improvement of the quality of urban compost prepared at mechanical compost plants (Gaur, 1983).

Constraints in Adoption

Farmers are well convinced with beneficial effect of compost in crop production as well as for sustainability in crop yields. However, there are number of constraints which hampers the adoption compost. Important constraints as pointed out by Jay *et al.* (1992) are listed below:

1. Competitive uses of organic materials such as dung cakes for domestic cooking fuel and sugarcane bagasse as a fuel in sugar factories and villages.
2. Involvement of labour in collection scattered organic materials and production of good quality of compost.
3. Compost prepare at the mechanical plants from city garbage are poor in plant nutrients and also contains uncompostable materials.
4. Proper technology either for composting or *in situ* incorporation of residues has not been popularised among the farmers.
5. Farmers don't make serious effects in preparation and conservation of compost which also leads to production of poor quality of compost.

References

Acharya, C.N. 1940. *Indian J. Agri. Sci.* 10, 448.

Acharya, C.N. and Subrahmanyan, V. 1939. *Indian J. Agri. Sci.* 9:741

Flower, G. 1927. *Pocha seeds*, Poona.

Gaur, A.C. 1983. In: *Proc. Int. Symp. on biological reclamation and land utilisation of urban wastes* (Eds F. Zuccom *et al.*) : 531.

Gaur, A.C. 1992. In: *Fertilizers organic manures, recyclable wastes and biofertilizers components of integrated plant nutrition* (Ed Tandon) : 36.

Gaur, A.C. *et al.* 1990. *Organic Manures*, ICAR, New Delhi pp. 159.

Gildyal, B.N.P. 1953. *Agra Univ. Research* 2:27.

Howard, A. and Wad, Y.D. 1931. *The waste products of Agriculture*, Oxford Univ. Press, England.

Kanwar J.S. 1982. *Trans. 12 Int. Congr. Soil Sci.* Planary session papers, New Delhi India.

Lad, V.S. *et al.* 1990. *Proc.* 9th *Int. Cong. Soc. Sym.* Technologists, New Delhi pp 503.

Mishra, M.M.1992. In: *Non-traditional sectors for fertilizer use* (Ed H.L.S. Tandon) Fertilizer Development & Consultation organisation, New Delhi, India.

Nambiar, K.K.M. & Abrol, I.D. 1989. *Festel News* 34(4):11.

National Commission on Agriculture 1976. Report, Government of India, Ministry of Agriculture & Irrigation, New Delhi, India.

Richards, H.S. & Hutchinson 1921. *J. Nin. Agri.* 28, 598.

Singh, R.N. 1970. *Notes on fertilizers & manures for B.Sc.(Ag.) students*, The national book house, Jeonimandi, Agra, India.

Somani, L.L. 1998. *Integrated plant nutrition*. Agrotech Publishing Academy, Udaipur.

Tiwari, V.N. *et al.* 1989. *Proc. National Aca. Sci. India*, 59B:109

Yawalkar, K.S., Agarwal, J.P. and Bokale, S. 1996. *Agri-Horticultural Publishing*, House, Nagpur.

Chapter 9

Compost Making: A Demonstration

F.M. Qureshi

Assoc. Prof. Ag. Chem. & Soil Science, RCA, Udaipur

Introduction

Compost making is done from agricultural organic wastes like straw, leaves, paddy husk, groundnut husk, sugarcane trash, bagasse, cattle dung, urine and city wastes like city garbages, night soil, sewage and sludge and vegetable matter. These materials undergo intensive decomposition during compost making under thermophillic and mesophillic conditions in heaps or pits with sufficient moisture. After decomposition these agricultural organic wastes yield a brown to dark brown coloured humified material in 4 to 6 months which contains valuable plant nutrients and organic matter which upon addition to soil improves physical and microbiological condition of the soil and increase plant growth.

The compost making is achieved by the action of different groups of micro organisms like heterotrophic micro organisms, bacteria, fungi, actinomycetes and protozoa. Biodegradation processes are carried out under aerobic as well as anaerobic conditions and carbon compounds are reduced to CO_2, H_2O and energy while proteins are reduced to ammonia and nitrate. Similarly organic sulphur and phosphates are converted to SO_4= and $Ca(HPO_4)_2$.

Factors Involved in Compost Making

The most important factors in compost making are:

1. C/N ratio
2. Blending of wastes
3. Moisture and aeration
4. Temperature
5. Reaction
6. Micro organisms involved
7. Use of inoculants
8. Calcium phosphate and destruction of pathogens

When compost making is carried out in heaps, the decomposition becomes mainly aerobic and decomposition rate is increased if periodical turnings are given and nitrogen source in the form of organic materials such as activated sewage sludge or organic residues richer in nitrogen (*e.g.* legume residue, water-hyacinth, slaughter house wastes, green leaves, waste of sugar etc.) are added. Similarly, composting process can be accelerated if raw materials are shredded into smaller pieces and C/N ratio of raw materials is kept around 30 which is desirable for efficient composting. Higher C/N ratio reduced the microbial activity and hence takes longer time to decompose organic material in absence of nitrogen, therefore, addition of nitrogen can hasten composting by lowering the ratio. Similarly, lower C/N ratio under unfavourable conditions cause increasing loss of ammonia. To overcome this loss, soil is sometimes added @ 5-10 per cent to reduce the moisture content and to absorb ammonia in low C/N ratio materials. During aerobic composting high moisture content should be avoided and 50-60 per cent moisture is regarded as optimum.

In India pioneering work in compost making was carried out by Howard and Wad at Indore and Fowler at Bangalore who standardised conditions for degradation of agricultural waste materials utilising dung and night soil as starters for promoting bacterial activity.

Indore Method of Composting

In this method of composting, agricultural waste materials are spread out and moistened with cowdung. Heaps of 4-6 meters length, one meter breadth and one meter height are built using these waste materials. Since the decomposition is aerobic, the rate of decomposition is rapid and high temperatures develop quickly. Brown homogeneous manure is ready for use in about three months when the material of the heaps is turned and moistened when required. Turning and moisturing cause more or less total disintegration.

Limitations of this method are that 40-50 per cent losses of initial organic matter and nitrogen take place due to aerobic process of decomposition. Similarly, this method of manure preparation involves considerable labour in building up the heap to proper shape and periodical turnings that are given. This becomes expensive and almost impractical where large quantities of materials have to be processed. However turnings of the material in the heaps could be avoided if adequate moisture level is maintained. The manure produced in this method resembles the traditional FYM in appearance and properties. The average composition of manure prepared by this method has been found to be 0.8 per cent nitrogen, 0.3 per cent phosphorus and 1.5 per cent potash.

Fowler gave the process of activated compost in which fresh raw materials are incorporated in an already fermenting heap so that large microbial population which is already established in the heap brings about quicker decomposition. The process usually known as Bangalore process is useful particularly where offensive materials like night soil are to be quickly and effectively disposed off.

Bangalore Process

In this method of composting different trenches of dimension 4.5×1.5×1.0 cu meter or 6.0m×2.0m×1.0m or still bigger size, are created which can take the dumpings of city waste and night soil for a year.

The trenches are dug in rows with a space of 1 to 5 meters between trenches. Roads of suitable width are provided between rows for the carts to approach and unload the materials inside the trenches. At first, the refuse is dumped into the trench and spread out with rakes to make a layer of 15 cm. Night soil or cow dung is then discharged over this and if necessary, spread out with long wooden spades in a layer of about 5 cm. This is then covered with a 15 cm layer of refuse or agricultural waste material. Night soil and refuse or cow dung and agricultural waste material thus follow in alternate layers until the pit is filled to 15 cm above ground level with a final layer of refuse or agricultural waste material on the top. This may be domeshaped and covered with a thin layer of soil.

The dumped materials in pits decompose largely in the absence of sufficient air except in the surface foot or so. This anaerobic decomposition is comparatively slow but markedly less wasteful. The difference in recovery of organic matter and nitrogen by this method as compared to the aerobic method in over ground heaps (Indore method) is given below for manure prepared from town refuse and night soil.

Table

Constituents	***Percentage recovery***	
	Heap	***Trench***
Organic	53	78
Nitrogen	54	74

High temperatures do not develop in the layers and since the material does not receive turnings disintegration into a homogeneous mass of manure does not take place though C/N ratio is reduced to less than 20:1 in about six months and manure is ready for use.

In absence of facilities for digging trenches, town refuse and night soil compost can be prepared in over ground heaps of one meter height, one meter width and any convenient length with refuse and night soil or agricultural waste and cow dung placed in alternate layers as in trenches and a final refuse/agricultural waste layer on the top. No turnings are required to the heaps and the material decomposes more quickly than in pits and can be used after three to four months.

Preparation of Synthetic Compost

In this method inorganic fertilizers are used as sources of nitrogen for decomposition of carbonaceous materials. Organic nitrogen in the form of dung, required by micro organisms, can be completely substituted by inorganic nitrogen compounds like ammonium sulphate and urea which are utilised equally well for decomposition and well fermented manure like FYM can be obtained.

Nitrogenous fertilizers in sufficient quantity are added to various organic waste materials to reduce the C/N ratio to about 30-40 per cent and then allow the material to be decomposed and disintegrated until the C/N ratio is reduced to 20:1. This process of compost making from organic wastes of wide C/N ratio is done with fertilizers like ammonium sulphate or urea - nitrogen is added to make up a total of 1.2 per cent on dry weight basis of the material. Thus, straw containing 0.4 per cent nitrogen requires an additional 0.8 per cent nitrogen equivalent to 4 kg ammonium sulphate or 1.75 kg urea per 100 kg of straw. For neutralising acidity, which may develop in this system, lime is added @ 5 kg/100 kg straw. The material to be composted is spread out in layers in a heap or pit and sufficiently moistened. To every layer of the organic material, fertilizer solution is sprinkled and then lime is sprayed. Super phosphate may also be added @ 5 per cent to increase phosphate contents of manure. The treatment is continued layerwise until the heap or pit is filled to size and allowed to decompose. The manure is ready for application in about 4-6 months and looks like FYM in its action on soil and plant growth.

Nitrogen Loss Control during Compost Making

Addition of superphate @ 5 per or mineral acid (HCL) @ 1 per cent conserves nitrogen in manure. Similarly materials like charcoal dust, saw dust, gypsum or soil itself when added @ 5-10 per cent reduce nitrogen losses of the manure considerably and superior quality manure is obtained.

Important Note

The organic manure usually prepared by farmers of our region has low percentage of nitrogen (about 0.5%) and there are low responses when they are applied to the soil as they are inadequate to make good the primary deficiency of nitrogen in our soils. Thus a low quality manure containing 0.5 per cent nitrogen and a C/N ratio of 20:1 can be treated with ammonium sulphate or urea solution to add 2 per cent more nitrogen and raise the total nitrogen content to 2.5 per cent. This would immediately reduce the C/N ratio to 8:1 and the enriched manure can then be utilised effectively. This method can utilise large quantities of other organic waste materials of wide C/N ratio like dry dung, paddy and groundnut husks, saw dust, tobacco waste, wheat chaff and any material in condition to be easily incorporate in soil. Enriched manures of the above type are processed and get ready in a short time thus eliminating composting and saving labour. Such enriched manures possess many advantages.

Preparation of Enriched Manures

1. Take requisite quantity of nitrogenous and other fertilizes.
2. Dissolve the fertilizers in sufficient water.
3. Add 100 ml of commercial hydrochloric acid per quintal of the final manure for controlling nitrogen loss.
4. Sprinkle the above solution of fertilizers and HCL on the calculated quantity of the organic material, mix thoroughly and dry in the sun.
5. Fill the dry enriched manure if required into bags and store for use.

Chapter 10

Chemical and Biological Enrichment of Compost

U.S. Rawat

Assoc. Prof., Dept. of Agri. Chem. & Soil Sc., RCA, Udaipur

Introduction

Organic wastes are valuable sources of plant nutrients if properly processed and converted to be used as manures. India with very large land area, having adequate sunlight and water has enormous potential of producing huge quantities of biomass through photosynthesis, via terrestrial, agricultural or aquatic pathways, out of which a part is consumed and rest is available for recycling, even the part, consumed by the living system is not fully utilised and unspent protion comes out as excreta. The manorial value of composted material varies depending upon the material used, method followed, conditions during composting and handling of composted material. Nutrient value of compost can be improved upon by integrating in with other sources while applying to field (Roy, 1992) or by supplementing either with chemicals or biological organism during composting. The quality of compost can also be improved by use of celluloselignin degrading micro-organism (Gaur, 1990).

Biological Enrichment

Biological enrichment and/or acceleration of compost can be achieved by the use of micro-organism which accelerates the rate of decomposition, which contributes towards nutrient enrichment and which improves the solubility of nutrients.

Composting involves the release of CO_2 or reduce C:N ratio which is accomplished by natural flora present in dung soil and plant residues. It can be accelerated by inoculating composting material with selected strains of fungi, actinomycetes etc.

Table 1

Effect of Fungal Inoculation on Decomposition

Treatment	***Sugarcane + Rash***		***Paddy Straw***	
	C:N Ratio	***% Loss***	***C:N Ratio***	***% Loss***
Control	35	57	33	58
Trichurus spiralis	26	67	25	69
Paecilomyces fusiporus	26	66	27	66
Aspergillus sp.	24	67	24	68
Cattle dung (10%)	25	66	23	65
Original material	124.5	-	82.7	-

Table 2

Effect of Inoculants on Decomposition, Nitrogen and Phosphorus Content

Treatment	***Loss in wt. %***	***Total N %***	***Citric Acid Soluble P (mg/g)***
Control (T_1)	42	1.33	1.24
Waste + RP (T_2)	51	1.45	1.84
Waste + *Paecilomyces fusisporus* (T_3)	57	1.60	0.99
T_3 + RP (T_4)	48	1.57	1.85
T_2+ *Aspergillus awamorii* (T_5)	59	1.62	2.12
Waste + *Azotobacter* (T_6)	59	1.75	1.17
T_5 + Azotobacter	49	1.63	2.09
T_4 + Azotobacter	55	1.65	1.64

Yadav *et al.* (1982) observed use of *Trichurus spiralis, Paecilomyces fusiporus* and *Aspergillus* spp. helped to produce compost with lower C:N ratio from sugarcane trash and rice straw. They also observed that cow dung was equally effective but required in large quantities (Table 1). Use of various fungi, in combination with *Azotobacter* and rock phosphate accelerated the rate of composting, nitrogen content and citric acid soluble P (Kappor *et al.,* 1983). Table 2 shows that waste + RP + *Penicillium fusisporus+Azotobacter* resulted in loss weight by 55 per cent, total nitrogen 1.68 per cent and citrate soluble P 1.64 mg/g compared to 42$, 1.33 and 1.24 mg/g under control.

Table 3

Changes C:N Ratio of Composting Sugarcane Trash and Response of Green Gram to Compost

Treatment	***C:N Ratio at Weeks***	***Nitrogenase Activity (Micro Mole of Acetylene/g/h)***	***Gran (g/pot)***
T_0	-	32	13.0
T_1	38.0	43	15.1
T_2	34.6	46	16.5
T_3	32.6	52	19.7
T_4	33.6	44	23.2
T_5	29.6	50	25.6
T_6	31.8	52	18.2
T_7	29.4	48	21.2
T_8	27.9	52	25.0
T_9	24.9	62	27.6
CD (0.5)	-	5.0	3.2

T_0 = Control, T_1 = Sungarcane trash, T_2 = ST + *Penicillum* sp., $T_3 = T_2$ = 1% MRP, $T_4 = T_2$ + PSB, $T_5 = T_4$ + 1% MRP, $T_6 = T_2$ + *Azotobcter,* $T_7 = T_6$ + %MRP, $T_8 = T_6$ + *Azotobacter,* $T_9 = T_8$ + 1% MRP.

In another study, Yadav *et al.* (1992) studied the composting of sugarcane trash in presence of *Penicillum,* sp. P. solubiliser, *Azotobacter* and rock phosphate and observed narrow C:N ratio at the end of 15 weeks (Table 3). They also observed better response of supplementation by green gram with respect to nitrogenase activity and grain yield. Patel and Bhandari (1992) observed higher release of phosphours from Udaipur rock phosphate when inoculated with *Bacillus megaterium* var phophaticum (Table 4). Improved C:N ratio, release of nutrients and improved microbial activity were observed during composting of mechanical plant compost, city garbage and rice straw (Mann *et al.,*1997). When inoculated with micro-organisms like *Aspergillus, Bacillus* spp., *Azotobacter, Paecilomyces fusiporus* etc.

Table 4

Release of Available Phosphorus, Heat Soluble Sulphur and DTPA Extractable Iron from Rock Phosphate (RP) and Pyrite Applied in Conjunction with FYM and Bacteria after 60 Days Period

Treatment	*P*	*S (mg kg^{-1})*	*Fe*
T_1 = Control	5.173	7.953	5.680
T_2 = SSP alone @ 7.8 (mg kg^{-1})	9.306	11.268	7.181
T_3 = RP alone @ 7.8 (mg kg^{-1})	7.552	8.559	6.079
T_4 = RP + Pyrite (1:0.5)	7.939	10.591	7.582
T_5 = RP + Pyrite (1:1)	8.326	11.975	9.785
T_6 = RP + Pyrite (1:2)	8.734	13.432	11.176
T_7 = RP + Pyrite (1:3)	9.211	15.165	12.843
S. Em ±	0.015	0.021	0.020
L.S.D. at 5%	0.043	0.061	0.058
F_0 = No FYM	7.353	10.597	8.400
F_1 = FYM @ 0.45 %	8.716	11.958	8.836
S. Em ±	0.008	0.011	0.011
L.S.D. at 5%	0.023	0.032	0.031
B_0 = No inoculation	7.983	11.255	8.590
B_1 = Inoculated @ 10^3 g^{-1} soil	8.086	11.300	8.646
S. Em ±	0.008	0.011	0.011
L.S.D. at 5%	0.023	0.032	0.031

Chemical Enrichment

There are many natural mineral which have low content of plant nutrients and are economically not suitable for fertilizer production like rock phosphate, pyrite and many byproducts, these materials when used as supplement to composting material, enrich the compost and have good agronomic values. Table 5 shows the chemical composition of compost and phosphocompost is better. The response of crops to phosphocompost are presented in Table 6 (Mishra *et al.,* 1989).

Table 5

Chemical Analysis of Composts

	Compost		*Phosphocompost*	
	0 Day	*90 Days*	*0 Day*	*90 Days*
O.C. %	46.2	29.1	34.2	22.6
Total nitrogen %	0.62	0.95	0.54	0.83
Total phosphorus %	0.265	0.382	2.35	3.21
Water soluble P (mg/g)	0.13	0.52	0.09	0.37
Citric acid (2%) soluble P (mg/g)	1.26	5.63	1.36	14.28

Table 6

Effect of Phosphocompost on the Yield of Crops (q/ha)

Treatment	*Wheat*	*Pigeon Pea*	*Green Gram*	*Cluster Bean*
Control	15.15	15.81	7.77	5.43
MRP	15.98	13.97	8.27	6.87
SSP	47.20	17.15	9.44	8.36
Phospocompost	45.72	17.49	9.68	8.21
Compost + RP	16.82	-	-	-

Chitdeshwar and Krishnasamy (1997) studied the nutrient content of Zn enriched and normal manures and their dynamics in soils (Table 7) and reported that enriched compost is better source of nutrient and responds.

Table 7
Characteristics of Organic Manures

Parameter	*Organic Manure*			*Zn-Enriched Manure*			
	FYM	*CCP*	*GLM*	*FYM*	*CCP*	*CCP + GLM*	*FYM GLM*
DTPA Micronutrient (mg kg^{-1})							
Zn	73.5	30.0	20.0	100.0	49.5	41.5	41.0
Fe	1437.0	3662.0	896.0	2000.0	2662.0	4300.0	4909.0
Mn	187.0	25.2	880.0	247.0	96.2	81.5	75.0
Cu	20.0	3.6	6.0	21.5	8.5	9.5	6.0

CCP = Compost Coir Path; GLM = Green Leaf Manure

Conclusion

Nutrient contents and agronomic value of composts can be improved by supplementing the composting materials. It helps in low grade minerals as a source of nutrient which otherwise are suitable. The composting period could be reduced by accelerators use like micro-organisms. Use of *Azotobacter* helps in enriching the compost with respect to nitrogen and thus reduces the C:N ratio.

References

Chitadeshwari, T. And Krishnasamy, R. 1997. *J. India Soc. Soil Sci.* 45:774.

Gaur, A.C. 1990. "Proc. Workshops on solid waste management and resource mobilisation," Kathmandu, Nepal. Volume B, pp 1.

Kapoor, K.K.; Yadav, K.S.; Singh, D.P.; Mishra, M.M. and Tauro, P. 1983. *Agric. Wastes* 5:125.

Manna, M.C.; Hazhra, H.N.; N.B. Sinha and T.K. Ganguly 1997. *J. Indian Soc. Soil. Science*, 45:831.

Mishra, M.M.; Kukreja, K.; Kapoor, K.K. and Bangar, K.C. 1989. In: *Soil micro-organism and crop growth* (Ed. L.L. Somani and S.C. Bhandari), Divyajyoti Prakashan, Jodhpur.

Patel, J.J. and Bhandari, S.C. 1992. In: *Proc. Int. Symp. Nutrient management for sustain productivity* (Ed. V. Beri, M.R. Chaudhary, P.S. Sidhu, N.S. Pasrich and M.S. Bajwa). Vol.II, 157.

Roy, R.N. 1992. In: *Fertilizers, organic manures, recyclable wastes and bio-fertilizers*. FDCO, New Delhi.

Yadav, K.; Prasad, D.; Prasad, C.R. and Mandal, K. 1992. *J. Indian Soc. Soil Sci.* 40:71.

Yadav, K.L.; Mishra, M.M. and Kapoor, K.K. 1982. *Agric. Wastes* 4:329.

Chapter 11

Green Manuring: A Source of Organic Carbon and Plant Nutrients

A.K. Vyas
Assoc. Prof., Dept. of Agronomy, RCA, Udaipur

Green manuring can be defined as practice of ploughing or turning into the soil undecomposed green plant tissues for the purpose of improving physical structure as well as fertility of the soil. Green manuring is mainly of two types:

Green Manuring *In Situ* - In this system, green manure crops are grown and buried in the same field which is to be green manured either as a pure crop or as intercrop with the main crop. The most common green manure crops grown under this system are sannhemp, dhaincha, guar, etc.

Green Leaf Manuring - This refers to turning into the soil green leaves and tender twings collected from shrubs and trees grown on bunds, wastelands and nearby forest areas. The common shrubs and trees are Glyricidia, dhaincha, karanj, etc.

The advantages generally attributed to green manuring are:

1. It adds organic matter to the soil.
2. Green manure crops return the plant nutrients taken up by the crop from deeper layers to the upper top soil.
3. Green manure crops hold plant nutrients that would otherwise be lost by leaching.

4. When leguminous plants like sannhemp, dhaindra, guar, etc. are used as green manure crops, they add atomospheric N into the soil for the succeeding crop.
5. It increases the microbial activity in the soil which are involved in the mineralisation of nutrients.
6. It increases the availability of certain plant nutrients like P, K, Ca, Mg, Fe, etc.

Source of Organic Carbon

Green manuring adds a significant amount of organic carbon into the soil. In other worlds, green manuring is done to add organic carbon into the soil and to improve the physical and chemical properties of soil. From Table 1 it is evident that green manuring adds a significant amount of green matter into the soil which after decomposition bring about a significant improvement in the organic carbon content of the soil.

Table 1

List of Common Leguminous Green Manure Crops

Name	***Botanical Name***	***Growing Season***	***Av. Yield of Green Matter (q/ha)***	***N (% on Green wt. Basis)***	***N Added (Kg/ha)***
Sannhemp	*Crotolaria juncea*	Kharif	152	0.43	84.0
Dhaincha	*Sesbania aculeta*	Kharif	144	0.42	77.1
Mung	*Vigna radiata*	Kharif	57	0.53	38.6
Cowpea	*V. sinensis*	Kharif	108	0.49	56.3
Guar	*Cyamopsis tetrogonoloba*	Kharif	144	0.34	62.3
Senji	*Melilotus alba*	Rabi	206	0.51	134.4
Kesari	*Lathyrus sativus*	Rabi	88	0.54	61.4
Berseem	*Trifolium alexandrinum*	Rabi	111*	0.43	60.7

* First two cuttings for fodder and green matter of third cutting is buried in the soil for green manuring.

Source: T.J. Mirchandani and A.R. Khan, 1952.

Source of Plant Nutrients

Green manuring serve as direct and indirect source of plant nutrients. Direct source in the sense that it adds some of the nutrients in major amount and some in minor quantities. Indirect in the sense that it helps in mobilisation and mineralisation of many plant nutrients either through increasing microbial activity or through moderation effect on soil pH

Improves N Supply

Normally green manure crops are leguminous and capable of fixing atmospheric N into the soil. Under different soil and climatic conditions, different crops can fix 40-100 kg N/ha. Leguminous crops add more N than non-leguminous crops. The extent of contribution of leguminous crops in N addition is given in Table 1. The foliage of wild leguminous plants/trees can also be used for green manuring. The contribution of some of the plants is given in Table 2.

Table 2

Chemical Composition of Wild Leguminous Plants/Trees

Name of Plants	*% (Dry wt. Basis)*			
	N	*P_2O_5*	*K_2O*	*CaO*
Cassia occidentalis	5.90	1.11	3.18	2.43
Prosopis juliflora	5.57	0.90	3.11	1.01
Sesbania aegyptiaca	4.00	0.43	2.41	2.62
Albizzia sp.	3.81	0.29	1.14	5.31
Cassia pumila	3.77	0.50	2.04	2.38
Tephrosia purpurea (wild indigo)	3.73	0.64	2.14	1.97
Melilotus indica (Senji)	3.36	0.49	1.53	2.49
Pongamia pinnata (karanj)	2.79	0.32	1.72	2.52

Source: Ambika Singh, 1974.

Besides, Glyricidia (*Glyricidia maculata*) is planted 183 cm apart on the borders of paddy fields or wastelands and it grows 180-300 cm in height. Under favourable soil and climatic conditions and gives annually two cuttings of 6.8 - 9.0 kg each of green leaves containing 3.0 per cent N on dry wt. Basis.

Wild dhaincha (*Seshania apeciosa*) seedlings are planted 10 cm apart. A border of 1 acre produces annually 907 kg of green leaves containing 2.2 per cent N on dry wt. Basis.

Wild Indigo (*Tephrosia purpurea*) green leaves contain 3.7 per cent N on dry wt. Basis.

Improves Supply of Major Nutrients

Besides supplying N, green manuring supply significant amount of other major elements as evident from Table 2. The chemical composition of leaves of wild leguminous plants/trees clearly shows that P_2O_5, K_2O, and CaO are present in considerable amount. Not only major nutrients, minor nutrients which are essential for plant growth and absorbed by the green manure crop for its growth return back to soil when the crop is turned into the soil.

Concentration of Nutrients at Soil Surface

Green manure crop improves the fertility of the surface soil by absorbing nutrients from deeper soil layers and bringing them to surface when they are turned into the surface soil.

Conservation of Nutrients in Soil

The nutrients are present in the organic forms in the green manure crops/plants which are not liable to loss through surface runoff, leaching, volatilisation, etc. Particularly N and K are liable to leaching but escape when added through green manuring.

Improves Availability of Nutrients

Green manuring improves the availability of P, K, Ca, Mg, Fe, Cu, Zn, etc. During decomposition of green manure plant material, some organic and inorganic acids are produced which bring down the soil pH and dissolve unavailable forms of nutrients. This temporary moderation of soil pH improves the availability of some nutrients. Green manuring increases the number and activity of useful micro-organisms which improve the availability of nutrients like N, P, S, etc.

References

Ambika Singh, 1974. "Utilising legumes in the nitrogen economy of soil. *Indian Farming*, 23(11): 5-9.

Mirchandani, T.J. and Khan, A.R., 1952. *Green manuring*, ICAR Review Series No. 6.

Chapter 12

Organic Farming and Crop Response and Quality of Products

L.L. Dhakar

Directorate of Extension Education, Udaipur

Introduction

The term organic, as applied to the farming systems, refers to the development of farm as an organic whole, a carefully integrated and balanced system, rather than to a unit which specifically utilises recycled organic matter, although the later interpretation also applies. During the 1950s and 60s organic farming was generally rejected as being an eccentric system with no place in the main stream of agriculture. More recently, particularly as the inherent weaknesses of conventional farming, chemically based systems have begun to appear, organic farming is increasingly being seen as an alternative to conventional farming. Studies are showing that organic farming is economically viable, productive environmentally benign and scientifically sound.

Organic farming is defined as a "production system which avoids or largely excludes the use of synthetic fertilizer, pesticide and growth regulators. The more widely used term organic farming describes two manor aspects of alternate agriculture—(1) The substitution of manures and organic matter instead of fertilizers, and (2) the biological pest control instead of chemical pest control.

Organic Farming in India

Reports of deletrious effects arising with the use of agro-chemicals was being observed by the Government of India for quite sometime. To study the viability of organic farming in India, a technical team constituted by the Ministry of Agriculture visited several research stations and farmers practising organic farming during 1993 and made the following observations: "The country at present is not in a position to eliminate completely he use of chemicals especially fertilizers. However, it would not be difficult and unrealistic to phase out the use of these chemicals systematically. For this, the doses of fertilizer need to be gradually reduced and be balanced by increasing the use of optimum quantity of organic materials and bio-fertilizers."

Organic Farming and Crop Responses

The agronomic value of an organic material is to increase the crop yield and quality. There is a considerable published information which verifies the beneficial effect of organic materials on crop yield, but very little on crop quality. Crop yield response to the addition of organic materials is highly variable and is dependent upon the crop, soil type, climatic conditions, management system, and the organic material used.

Table 1

Performance of Rice under Different Farming System

S. No.	*Farming System*	*Plant Height (cm)*	*No. of Grains per Particle*	*Grain Yield (t/ha)*
1.	Conventional farming (160:60:80)	103.4	85.9	7.43
2.	Intermediate farming (80:30:40 plus 6.6 t/h organic compost)	97.2	76.9	6.22
3.	Organic farming (A) (composted log manure @ 13.3 t/ha)	100.4	76.8	5.70
4.	Organic farming (B) (composted chicken manure @ 13.3 t/ha)	109.4	86.3	7.43

Source: Sun, P.M.H. & Hseik, S.C. In-*Sustainable agriculture for the Asian and Pacific region.* FFTC Book Series No. 44, pp 59.

In order to evaluate feasibility of organic farming in Taiwan, experiments were carried out to compare rice yield from conventional farming (chemical) with those from organic farming as well as an intermediate farming system (a mixture of chemical and organic material). A sugar vinegar microbial solution together with other natural pesticides were used for pest control. Results of the experiments revealed that rice yield obtained in organic farming (B) was at par with conventional farming (Table 1).

Experiments conducted in Japan revealed that application of organics (cattle manure, coir dust and leaves of perennial legumes) along with effective micro-organisms produced minimal increase in the yield of selected food crops in first two seasons. With time, the beneficial effects were observed in terms of enhanced yield.

Organic Manures and Crop Response

Organic manures such as FYM and compost are low in major plant nutrients as compared to chemical fertilizers. Well composted organic manure contains appr. 0.5 - 1.0 per cent N, 0.2 - 0.3 per cent P_2O_5 and 0.5 per cent K_2O. Ten tons of compost will provide 50-100 kg N, 20-30 kg P_2O_5 and 50 kg K_2O, out of which 15-30 kg N, 10-15 kg P_2O_5 and 35 K_2O will be available to crops during first year of application and the rest become available to the subsequent crop.

Long-term experiments (10 yrs) on effect of fertilizers, and FYM and BGA was conducted at Samastipur (Bihar). Results of the experiment revealed that yield of rice under FYM, BGA, and BGA + FYM were significantly higher than under no manure. Interaction effect of fertilizer and manure revealed that additional increase in grain yield occurred when fertilizers were applied in conjunction with FYM, BGA and FYM + BGA. It is interesting that grain yield of rice, wheat and winter maize under 50 per cent NPK + FYM + BGA and 100 per cent NPK alone was almost similar. This indicates that 50 per cent nutrients in fertilizers could be substituted with long-term application of 10 t FYM + 13 kg algae crust ha^{-1} in conjunction with 50 per cent NPK. Besides nutritional effects, FYM and/or BGA helped in improvement of physical environment, thereby stimulated root growth and thus increased the capacity of plants for efficient utilisation of nutrient and water. This resulted in higher grain yields of crops (Mishra and Sharma, 1997).

Experiment conducted at Mohanpur (W.B.) revealed that yield of rice improved significantly when the rice was fertilized with 75 per cent recommended dose of N, P(SSP) and K along with FYM (10 t/ha). The level of productivity of crop in the treatment was as good as the productivity obtained in the treatment 100 per cent N, P (SSP) and K as chemical fertilizer. It might be due to be the fact that organic manure increased the efficiency of applied fertilizers (Mandal *et al.,* 1994).

A long-term field experiment was conducted on sandy loam soil at Sriganganagar. The results of the experiment showed that full dose of NPK was found to be on par with ½ FYM + ½ NPK dose and full FYM in influencing seed cotton yield. Application of FYM increased field capacity by 18.1 per cent and decreased infiltration rate by 40.3 per cent over control. FYM also significantly increased Zn and Mn over rest of treatments. This might be the reason that seed cotton yield under FYM (100%), and FYM (50%)+ NPK (50%) was on par with 100 per cent NPK (Mathur, 1997).

Velayudhan *et al.* (1996) reported that organic wastes significantly increased the grain and straw yields of rice over control. Increase in grain yield on incorporation of organic wastes ranges from 4.2 to 10.0 q/ha. The results establish the usefulness of addition of locally available organic wastes for improving and sustaining the productivity of crops under saline soil conditions.

Gaur and Mukherjee (1979) reported that incorporation of straw in sandy loam soil, one week before sowing improved nodulation and pod yield of groundnut by 95.5 per cent with 5t straw/ha. Besides, there was residual effect with 10 t of straw per ha which significantly increased grain yield of succeeding wheat.

Green Manures and Crop Response

Green manuring has proved a feasible and reliable practice to improve the productivity of important cropping system and soil fertility as well.

Experiment conducted at Pantnagar (U.P.) reveals that different levels of nitrogen and green manure of *Sesbania* significantly increased grain yield of rice over control. Application of 90 kg N/ha was as good as green manuring by *S. rostrata* and *S. cannabina.* Integrated management of *Sesbania* and prilled urea saved more than 60 per cent of chemical nitrogen. *Sesbania* green manuring or with prilled urea supplies NH_4^+-N to the rice crop through continuous mineralisation of organic N, thus increase nitrogen use efficiency, ultimately giving higher yield (Mahapatra and Sharma, 1997). Similarly, four years study at Ludhiana showed that green manuring with sunhemp significantly decreased soil pH and increased organic matter of soil and water retention capacity of the soil. All these beneficial effects of green manuring increased wheat grain yield in all the successive years (Ghuman *et al.,* 1997).

Bio-Fertilizers and Crop Response

A positive effect of bio-fertilizers like N-fixers, phosphate solubilisers and micorrhiza's on yield of crops was reported by many workers. Balasubramanian and Palannippan (1994) reported that use of microbial inoculants alone and in combination with FYM favoured groundnut production over control. Similarly, Chauhan *et al.* (1997) reported that inoculated mustard crop receiving moderate level of N (30kg/ha) gave similar grain yield as the crop receiving higher dose of N (60 kg/ha) but uninoculated. This clearly showed that fertilizer N requirement of the crop was reduced when it was inoculated with bio-fertilizers. Favourable effect of inoculation could be attributed to increase in N supply due to N-fixation ability of bacteria's.

Organic Farming and Quality of Product

Continuous use of chemicals (fertilizers, pesticides etc.) in agriculture is contaminating food and feeds and thus, causing health hazards to human and livestock. Health hazard associated with heavy metals entering the food chain through fertilizers is seeking attention of human beings nowadays.

Table 2

Lead and Cadmium Content (mg/kg) of Fertilizers

Fertilizers	*Lead*	*Cadmium*
Urea	4	1
CAN	200	6
Muriate of potash	88	14
DAP	188	109
SP	609	187
RP	1135	303
RP	1135	303

There is a very little information available on beneficial effects of organic materials on crop quality. Organic materials and bio-fertilizers increase protein content in grains of crop which resulted from higher uptake of N by crop and accumulated in grains (Patel and Patel, 1991 and Takankhar *et al.,* 1997).

References

Balasubramanian, P. and Palaniappan, 1994. *Indian J. Agron.* 39:131-33.

Chauhan, D.R.; Paroda, S. and Ram M. 1996. *Indian J. Agron.* 41:620-632.

Dahama, A.K. 1996. *Organic farming for sustainable agriculture.* Agro Botanical Publishers.

Gaur. A.C. and Mukherjee, D. 1979. *Indian J. Agric. Sci.* 49:978-980.

Ghuman, B.S.; Sur H.S and Lal, K. 1997. *J. Indian Soc. Soil Sci.* 45:99-103.

Mahapatra, B.S. and Sharma, G.L. 1996. *Indian J. Agron.* 41:262-29.

Mathur, G.M. 1997. *J. Indian Soc. Soil Sci.* 45:288-92.

Mishra, V.K. and Sharma, R.B. 1997. *J. Indian Soc. Soil Sci.* 45:84-88.

Mondal, S.S.; Mondal, T.K.; Dandapat, S. and Sarkar, S. 1994. *Indian J. Agron.* 39:116-18.

Patel, R.S. and Patel, Z.G. 1991. *Indian J. Agron.* 36(3) : 419-20.

Sum, P.M.H. and Hseik, S.C. In - *Substainable agriculture for the Asian and Pacific region.* FFTC Book Series No. 44, pp 59.

Takankhar, S., Mane, S.S., Kamble, B.G. and Indukar, B.S. 1997. *J. Indian Soc. Soil Sci.* 45 : 394-395.

Velayudham, K.; A.; Veerabadran, V.; Manoharan, S. and Bala, R. 1996. "Alwar Arunachalam," *Indian J. Agron.* 41 : 584-85.

Chapter 13

Agronomic Practices under Organic Farming to Increase Soil Productivity

M.S. Shaktawat

Prof. & Head, Depth. of Agronomy, RCA, Udaipur

In recent decades, agriculture has played a vital role in development strategies of our country through meeting food demands of ever increasing population and improving welfare of masses by generating employment and income. The recent technological advances and their adoption ushered into "green revolution." But at the same these have intensified environmental and soil degradation, shrinkage in diversity of natural resources, diminishing biodiversity and social in equability. Thus recognising these negative impacts a series of alternatives have been proposed to achieve sustainable development in agriculture so that long-term effects of development do not damage rightful heritage of future generation. More specifically "sustainable agriculture is the successful management of resources for agriculture to satisfy human needs, while maintaining or enhancing the quality of environment and conserving natural resources." In broader sense agriculture is considered to be sustainable if it is ecological sound, economically viable, socially just, humane and adaptable.

In recent years to achieve sustainability in agricultural development, there has been resurgence of interest in several alternative productive technologies, out of which "organic farming" is considered to be one.

Though this system is ancient in principle but recently proposed by Sir Albert Howard before First World War. This is a production system which avoids or largely excludes the use of synthetically compounded fertilizer, pesticide, growth regulators and animal feed additives etc. Thus by and large it relies upon crop residues, organic manures, green manuring, mechanical cultivation and aspects of biological pest control to maintain soil productivity for supplying nutrients and to control insects pests and weeds.

Though this concept has gained wider acceptance in the recent past but in India, the importance of organic manures in cultivation of crop was well appreciated since era of early civilisation as it has been well documented in *Rigveda*. Eloborate injections are also descrtibed in *Arthshastra*, *Brihatsamita* and *Agnipuran* regarding use of animal excreta bones, fish etc. as manures. In wider sense organic agriculture can also be considered a dynamic system of food and fiber production that systematically pursues following principles to achieve sustainability of natural resources base:

- Organise the production of crops and livestock and management of farmer resources so that they harmonise rather than conflict with natural system.
- Use and development of appropriate technology based upon understanding of biological system.
- Achieve and maintain soil fertility for optimum production by relying primarily on renewable resources/incorporation of natural processes (nutrient cycling, biological N fixation, phosphate solubilisation and pest predater relationship) in a agriculture production.
- Use diversification to pursue optimum production.
- Aim for achieving optimal nutritional value of staple food.

These principles clearly underlines wide deviation from present agricultural production system which is centred around:

- To substitute monoculture and continuous culture for crop rotation and diversified agriculture (replacing natural communities to artificially supported productive communities).
- To use genetically more uniform plants having narrow genetic base.

- To use inorganic fertilizers rather than organic manures/green manuring etc. (Compensate loss in soil fertility, depletion of nutrients and alteration in soil structure through use of fertilizer/soil conditioner).
- Use of herbicides and pesticides to combat weeds and pest rather than more complex biological control mechanism.

Technologies for Organic Sustainable Farming

The four basic elements of crop farming systems i.e. Rotation, tillage, fertility management and pest control are interwoven, interdependent and also dramatically affected by specific soils, climate and market situations.

Adoption of Efficient Crop Rotation/Cropping System

Currently in most of areas continuous cropping or monoculture is practised to ensure stable/optimal yields and maximum returns. However long-term experiments have clearly shown following potential hazards to long-term sustainability centring on interference with natural soil processes.

- Repeated use of fertilizers and pesticides in continuous row crop farming can suppress soil fertility.
- Decrease soil productivity, because of compacted soil structure, reduce ion exchange capacity and inhibit microbial activity.
- Destroy natural predators of crop pests.
- Increase erosion and leaching of chemicals to ground water.
- Intensified specific weed problem such as grassy weeds in continuous rice-wheat system.

Thus to increase productive capacity of land and to prevent its deterioration it necessary to restructure cropping patterns according to production environment, capacity of land and resources, to obtain maximum return without deteriorating soil, water and environment. The main principles in sequencing of crops should be to build soil productivity and to interrupt normal sequence in lives of pests which can be attained through:

- Following N-fixing legumes with higher uses of N.
- Preceding a slow growing, non-competitive corps with weed suppressing crop.

- Alternating deep and shallow rooted crops.
- Employing weed suppressing alletopathic crop such as sorghum/oats etc.
- Allowing sufficient time interval before repeating a crop which is vulnerable to insect and diseases.

Adoption of Reduced/Conservation Tillage for Restoring Soil Productivity and Conservation of Soil Moisture

Tillage is the mechanical manipulation and tillage system refers to sequence of operations that manipulates soils to produce a crop. Under conventional system, clean tillage (turn over of whole plant residues) is followed through ploughing field several times. This helps in maintaining optimum tilth for better germination and suppression of weeds. However, the excessive tillage have negative impacts on soil fertility as it enhance soil erosion, leaching and gaseous loss of nutrient, restrict build up of organic matter and several other physical properties of soils.

In recent years, concept of "conservation and reduced tillage" have been advocated with the main objectives to maintain plant residues on soil surface, reducing cost of tillage operation and restoring physico-chemical properties of soils. But under Indian condition still it is not practised due to non-availability of animal tractor drawn implements for planting under reduced tillage/ridge tillage/no till situations.

Appropriate Management Practices for Sustainable Nutrient Management

The major effects of intensive agriculture during the last three decades are manifested in erosion of soil fertility in terms of depletion of nutrients and organic matters. Increasing complexity of nutritional and environmental related problem (soil water and air pollution) have necessitated to evolve alternative measures for restoring soil fertility on sustainable basis. In this approach "Integrated nutrient management" is considered most appropriate under Indian conditions and involves following aspects:

Efficient Recycling of Farm Residues/Byproducts/Organic Waste

Organic fertilizers/manures is a wide term which includes manures made from cattle dung, excreta of other animals, crop residues and other byproducts of agriculture like oil cakes, slaughter house waste, poultry manure etc. These play an important role in maintaining physico-chemical and biological properties of soils. These are considered a good source of nutrient showing slow releasing capacity but have limitation of its application because of large volume and low nutrient content. The adoption of appropriate technology for their collection, conservation and utilisation can help in improving their efficiencies. Recently technologies have been also developed to upgrade nutrient content of compost and FYM and also hasten their composting process.

(1) use of accelater/inoculants,

(2) enrichment of compost by bio-inoculants such as N-fixing bacteria and P- solubilising fungi,

(3) Vermi-composting: In recent years "vermin-culture biotechnology" which deals with utilising working strength of earthworms on large scale to draw multiferous benefits for agriculture gaining momentum. However, there is need for standardisation of "vermi composting" because when the worms decompose externally added refuse increase fertility but as the same time deplete soil reserves. A major advantage of earthworm activity is that they work as living "ploughs," open up the soil for greater aeration, water retention and root development and hence promote water and nutrient absorption.

Efficient Recycling/Utilisation of Crop Residues

Crop residues with potential annual availability over 300 m tonnes are a major source of nutrients but only one-third of total estimates are available for direct recycling into soils. On an average cereal straw contains 0.5 per cent N, 0.64 per cent P_2O_5 and 1.5 per cent K_2O. Thus indicating supply of 1.13, 1.41 and 3.54 million tonnes of N, P_2O_5 and K_2O respectively. Even if 50 per cent of these are utilised as feed the rest can be properly utilised through compost, by way of mulch or direct turn in soils.

Restructuring Cropping Sequence/Land Use Planning for Green Manuring

It is a practice of turning/ploughing of undecomposed green plant tissues for improving physical structure as well fertility of soils.

Most of N brought by leguminous green manuring crops is a net gain as it is fixed from air but other nutrients are absorbed from soil reserves. Though this practice is ancient but in recent times is diminishing in spite of its technical merits. The requirements of land, labour and cash inputs limits its adoption at farm level. Green manuring crops can be planted in different combinations and configurations in time and space.

(1) Green manuring *in situ*: In this system green manure crops like sunhemp, dhaincha, clusterbean etc. are grown and buried in same field,

(2) Green leaf manuring: It refers to turning of green leaves of plants/trees grown on bunds, wasteland nearly forest area in fields. The common shrubs use are Glyricidia, sesbania species and karanj.

Extensive and Efficient Use of Bio-Fertilizers

These are preparations containing or latent cells of efficient strains of micro organisms capable of nitrogen fixation/P solubilisation. Bio-fertilizers are important components of INM but 90 per cent of their role is confined to nitrogen needs (biological N-fixation). These bacteria convert the nitrogen gas of atmosphere into ammonium which can be used by plants. Annual N-fixation on earth surface is estimated around 139 m tonnes annually while share of Indian soils can be put at 3.4 m tonnes. N-fixing bacteria can be divided into symbiotic, non-symbiotic and associated symbionts, symbiotic system : Rhizobium legume symbiosis; Non-symbiotic (free living) Azotobacter, Azospirillum, Blue green algae, Azolla; Phosphate solubilising micro-organism : PSB, PSP, DSF which solubilise insoluble inorganic phosphatic compounds including rock phosphate.

Limitations of Bio-Fertilizers

Poor quality control, poor transport and storage facility at field level and inconsistent field performance are command to be some of constraints which restricts their under acceptance at farm level.

Despite several technological options, still there is non-existence of blue print of sustainable agricultural production system having regional/ecological specificity. Some of the limitations/constraints to develop a comprehensive system for each microfarming situation seems to be:

- Agronomic principles cannot be separated from the economic and philosophical goals of the individual farmer/farm.
- Because of site/crop/ecological specificity the best results with adoption will vary from farm to farm.
- Conversion from present farming to sustainable system is a long-term project - a matter of several years rather than months.

Chapter 14

Management of Productivity of Orchards under Organic Farming

Shafaat Mohammed
Dept. of Horticulture, RCA, Udaipur

Introduction

Productivity is a function of fertility in interaction with the environment and management skills of the farmers. Management of productivity especially of orchards under organic farming assumes significance at a time when productivity is not being properly managed despite reckless use of fertilizers and pesticides. Indiscriminate use of inorganic fertilizers result in the nutrient imbalances which encourages continuous build up of nutrients that remain unutilised by growing crops. The leftover nutrients are the principal cause of the fertilizer related environmental pollution. For example, 'P' can cause eutriphication of lakes and rivers whereas unused 'N' can lead to groundwater pollution (as nitrate) or promote breakdown of protective ozone layer (as nitrons oxide) which shields the earth against harmful effects of UV radiation.

In view of the deterioration in the productivity of the orchard and in the environment there is a need to adopt organic farming system for the production of orchards crops. Organic farming is a production system which avoids or largely excludes the use of synthetically compounded fertilizers, pesticides, growth regulators etc. To the maximum possible extent organic farming systems rely upon crop rotation, crop residues animal manures, legumes, green manures, off farm organic wastes, mechanical cultivation, mineral bearing rocks and aspects of biological pest control to maintain soil productivity and to supply plant nutrient and to control insects, weeds and other pests. Thus organic farming system can be adopted to manage the productivity of orchards.

Present Status of Productivity

India is the second largest producer of orchard (fruit) crops in the world next only to Brazil. However, with its growing population, it is not in a position to meet the recommended per capita consumption norms. Fruits such as mango, banana, citruns, guava, and papaya are cultivated throughout the country (Table 1). Cultivation of apple sineapple, grapes, sapota is restricted to certain pockets. From the data concerning yield potential presented in Table 2 it becomes quite clear that productivity of orchards's very low. For example, productivity of citrus is only 8.06, and there is a potential to be raised to 30. Similarly, productivity of many fruits can be increased manifold. There are immense possibilities to achieve such manifold increases in the productivity of orchards under organic farming system.

Table 1

Area and Production of Fruits

Crop	***Area (lakh ha)***	***Production (lakh tonnes)***	***Productivity***
Mango	11.36	92.23	8.11
Banana	3.96	104.59	26.40
Citrus	3.69	29.79	8.06
Apple	1.91	11.68	6.11
Guava	1.12	12.04	10.77
Pineapple	0.59	8.58	14.45
Litchi	0.53	2.60	4.87
Papaya	0.47	8.03	16.94
Grapes	0.34	6.53	19.20
Sapota	0.30	4.23	13.75
Others	7.74	49.20	6.35
Total	32.05	329.55	10.28

Table 2
Yield Potential of Fruit Crops

Crop	*Present Yield*	*Potential*
Mango	8.11	15
Banana	26.40	58
Citrus	8.06	30
Apple	6.11	30
Pineapple	14.45	85
Sapota	13.75	80
Guava	10.77	20
Papaya	16.94	80
Grapes	19.20	25
Ber	5.00	20
Passion fruit	4.50	15
Others	10.28	42

Source: Yadav (1997) search for quality, cultivars. The Hindu Survey of India Agriculture.

Management of Orchard Productivity under Organic Farming

There are three main aspects *i.e.* management of nutrition, water and diseases under organic farming to raise the productivity of orchards.

Nutrient Management

Nutritional requirement of orchard crops under organic farming has to be met from the organic sources and use of inorganic sources must be avoided. There are number of organic sources which can be used to meet the nutritional requirements of fruits. Application of FYM, composted urban compost, sewage and sludge and night soils assumes special significance. Green manuring by green leaf, legumes and crop residues can be used to supply nutrients. Table 3 indicates nutrient contents of some of the organic manures ehich could be supplied to the orchard. The other organic sources of nutrients which can be used to augment and to maintain fertility levels of soils are vermicompost, bio-fertilizers and michorhizae.

Recycling of fallen leaves in the orchard may also become are important source of nutrients.

Table 3

Nutrient Content of Some Organic Manures

Manure	**Percentage Content**		
	N	P_2O_5	K_2O
Cattle dung (fresh)	0.3-0.4	0.1-0.2	0.1-0.3
Night soil (fresh)	1.0-1.6	0.8-1.2	0.2-0.6
Poultry manure (fresh)	1.0-1.8	0.8-1.2	0.2-0.6
Sewage sludge (dry)	2.0-3.5	1.0-5.0	0.2-0.5
Cattle urine	0.9-1.2	tr	0.5-1.0
Human urine	0.6-1.0	0.1-0.2	0.2-0.3
Crop-Residues			
Banana dry	0.61	0.12	1.00
Cotton	0.44	0.10	0.66
Sorghum	0.40	0.23	2.17

Water Management

Different methods are used by grower to irrigate crops. This ranges from watering individual plants from a can of water to highly automated irrigation through centrally controlled system. However, form the point of wetting the soil, these methods can be grouped under five headings:

a. Flood irrigation
b. Furrow irrigation
c. Sprinkler irrigation
d. Sub-surface irrigation
e. Localised irrigation (crop irrigation)

Among these methods drip irrigation under orchard conditions seems to be efficient method under organic farming system. Because in this method the application rate of water is adjusted to meet evapotranspiration needs so that percolation losses are minimised when compared with other systems under organic farming approach, the main advantages of drip irrigation seem to be:

- increased crop growth and yield achieved by optimising the water, nutrients and air-regimes in the root zone,
- high irrigation efficiency - no canopy interception, wind drift or conveyance losses and minimal drainage losses,
- minimal contact between farm workers and effluent,
- low energy requirements—the trickle system—requires a water pressure of only 100-300 k Pa (1-3 bar),
- low labour requirements - the trickle system can easily be automated, even to allow combined irrigation and fertilization *i.e.* fertigation.

Disease and Pest management

Organic farming emphasises use of biopesticides for insect, pest and disease management, bipesticides are the natural plant products that belong to the socalled secondary metabolities which includes thousands of alkaloids, terpenoids, pneholics and minor secondary chemicals. Botanical insecticides for example—Neem oil and other neem products are ecologically and environmentally safer and generally affect the behaviour and physiology of insect rather than killing them. Among the botanical insecticides neem has gained maximum attention as all parts of neem possess insecticidal property but seed kernal is the most active. Neembark, leaf, fruit and oil as well as extracts with various solvents especially ethanol have been found to exhibit activity against insectspests. Neem products appear to be quite promising against such hefarious pests as *S. Gregaria, L. Migratoria, H. Armigera, S. Litura and P. Xylostella.*

Conclusion

As explained above, the productivity of the orchards under organic farming may be maintained and in fact productivity can be raised if techniques described to monitor the nutritional and water requirements of orchards can be adopted. Similarly, diseases and pests can be controlled by using biopesticides rather than chemical pesticides.

Chapter 15

Organic Farming and Its Long-Term Effect on Soil Properties

B.L. Jain
National Bureau of Soil Survey and Land Use Planning, Regional Centre, Udaipur

Introduction

Intensive agriculture has manifested its effect in erosion of soil fertility in terms of depletion of soil nutrients and organic matter. Recently decline in yields in intensively cultivated areas has been observed. Continuous use of inorganic fertilizers has resulted in deficiency of secondary and micronutrients, deteriorating soil tilth, decreased organic matter affecting physical, chemical and biological condition of soil. Fortunately there is growing interest in promoting sustainable agriculture which rely on biological resources (Meelu, 1996). Crop residues, organic manure, legumes and green manure maintain organic matter and physical condition of soil to supply nutrients. Long-term influence of organic farming system on soil properties are discussed below.

Effects of Crops and Crop Sequences

Vegetal cover of crops affects physical properties of soil by providing protection against rain drops, improved granulation, porosity, organic matter production and root activity. Crops vary in their effect on soil structure and other soil properties.

Leguminous Crops

Legumes in cropping sequence add nitrogen and improve soil structure. Legumes contribute to good soil tilth, through addition of organic matter in roots and tops and increased production of organic matter by subsequent crops. Clover, guar and berseem manifests loose granular structure with increased water stable aggregates. Legumes also improve organic matter, soil aggregation and physical properties *viz*., bulk density, moisture retention and available water capacity. Incorporation of legumes in crop rotation reduces use of phosphatic fertilizers and organic manures.

Non-Leguminous Crops

The degradation of soils structures becomes severe with intensively tilled row crops like potato, maize, wheat, etc. Continuous cropping of potato reduces porosity and available water capacity. Maize, potato and wheat decrease organic matter and deteriorate soil structure. Cotton and pea though decrease organic matter yet improve soil structure. Sugarcane increases organic matter content, improve structural status and water retention of soil.

Grasses in rotation improve soil structure and nitrogen reserve of soils. Continuous grass is more effective than annual dressing of FYM in improving soil nitrogen. Grasses also increase hydraulic conductivity and decrease bulk density.

Good cropping sequence includes enough grass and legumes to reduce soil and water loss, reduce leaching of plant nutrients, maintain organic matter status, improve soil structure, and increase the yield of crops in rotation. Rotating crops provide efficient nutrient cycling.

Green Manuring

Legumes as cover crops and green manure result in higher organic matter, nitrogen and biologically available potassium. It has better capacity to store nutrients and water, larger microrganism population, and greater polysaccharides. Green manuring / leguminous crops in rotation, adds 40 to 50 Kg N/ha and restores fertility. Intercropping/mixed cropping of leguminous crops soybean, pigeonpea with high yielding sorghum/pearl millet are most remunerative and restore fertility. Green manuring influences soil physical properties, helps in formation of water stable aggregates, reduce bulk density, increase water holding capacity, total porosity and permeability. Aggarwal *et al.* (1997) reported low bulk density, vigorous root growth, high hydraulic conductivity and percolation rate under green manured plots of clay loam soils with rice-wheat rotation and high yield. Green manuring can be main source of plant nutrients in sustainable agriculture, enhance soil productivity and improve soil physical condition.

Table 1

Treatment	*Bulk Density ($g\ cm^{-3}$)*	*Hydraulic Conductivity (10^{-6} cm sec^{-1})*	*Percolation Rate (10^{-6} cm sec^{-1})*
Control	1.60	1.36	0.33
Green manure	1.46	2.64	0.56

Crop Residue

Crop residue recycling is environmentally sound practice for sustainable agriculture, source of multiple nutrients and improves soil characteristics. Bullakki and Badanur (1994) reported improvement in Vertisol soils by crop residue incorporation. Sorghum alone or in combination with subabue incorporation. Sorghum alone or in combination with subabul increased infiltration rate, reduced bulk density, increased water stable aggregates, organic carbon and available water storage capacity. Improvement in infiltration rate of vertisol is attributed to improved soil physical condition as result of high soil organic matter. Crop residue incorporation (Subabul + Safflower, Wheat, Bajra, Guar), enhance water content at 33 Kpa and 1500 Kpa and increases organic carbon content.

Table 2

Crop Residue	***O.C. (%)***	***B.D. $g\ cm^{-3}$***	***Infiltration Rate cm hr^{-1}***	***W.S.A. > 0.25 m (%)***	***Water Retention (%)***	
					33 kPa	***1500 kPa***
Control	0.43	1.35	0.15	43.2	29.7	21.8
NPK	0.48	1.37	0.14	42.4	30.3	22.1
Sorghum	0.55	1.17	0.21	50.6	33.8	22.7
Subabul	0.68	1.24	0.40	48.8	33.0	22.8
Sorghum+ Subabul	0.58	1.27	0.36	51.1	34.8	23.2

Incorporation of crop residues/green manure increases soil organic carbon, water stable aggregates, mean weight diameters, infiltration and reduced bulk density of soil and improve soil physical conditions.

Organic Manure

Bulky organic manures in addition to their effect on soil fertility and microbial activity influence soil physical properties such as structure, porosity, bulk density and water retaining and transmitting properties of soils. Building up of organic matter of soil also improves soil aggregation and related properties. Addition of FYM increases field capacity and permeability and have beneficial effect on moisture retention and water stable aggregates. FYM increases water stable aggregates due to polysaccharides formed during decomposition of organic residues by microbial activity and cementing activity of bacteria and fungi.

Unmanured and N treatment soils had low water retention and lower yields. Reduced crop residues including root matter and poor growth result in poor accumulation of organic matter in soils leading to poor soil physical condition. Incorporation of FYM improves soil physical properties like bulk density, aggregate stability, water retention and hydraulic conductivity. Lowering of bulk density by incorporation of FYM indicates improvement in soil physical properties. FYM application appreciably improves mean weight diameter suggesting appreciable improvement in soil structure and physical properties of soil.

Long Term Experiments: Case Study

Sandy Soils

In torripsamment soils of Sriganganagar application of FYM in long-term trial (10 years) improved soil properties (Mathur 1997) towards sustainable productivity. Application of FYM increased field capacity by 18.1 per cent, decreased infiltration rate by 40.3 per cent likely due to decrease in non-capillary porosity and increase in total porosity.

Table 3

Treatment	*Bulk Density g cm^{-3}*	*Water Retention*		*Infiltration Rate 10^{-5} cm sec^{-1}*
		1500 Kpa (m^3 m^{-3})	*33 Kpa (m^3 m^{-3})*	
Control	1.47	0.045	0.31	1.40
NPK	1.48	0.045	0.27	1.16
NPK + FYM	1.42	0.050	0.32	0.82

FYM incorporation decreased bulk density, due to enhanced organic carbon, more pore space and soil aggregation. Effect of bulk density and aggregation is reflected in their effect on hydraulic conductivity and water intake rate. Application of FYM has favourable effect on hydraulic conductivity. Addition of FYM improved water movement in fine textured soils through the formation of large soil aggregates, while it reduced the water movement in coarse textured soils through reduction in non-capillary porosity thereby moderating both the adverse soil conditions.

Black Soils

In vertisols of Dharwar, Karnataka application of FYM/green manuring decreased bulk density, increased infiltration rate, water stable aggregates, porosity, water retention characteristics and maximum water holding capacity (Bullakki and Badanur, 1997). This improvement is attributed to increase in organic matter status of soil and improved soil structure.

Table 4

Treatment	*BD gcm^{-3}*	*I.R. Cmhr^{-1}*	*WSA %*	*Water Retention*		*WHC (%)*	*OC (%)*
				33 Kpa (m^3 m^{-3})	*1500 Kpa (m^3 m^{-3})*		
Control	1.42	2.0	39.6	0.32	0.17	43	0.37
NPK	1.45	1.9	38.9	0.34	0.19	47	0.48
FYM	1.30	4.5	48.2	0.37	0.23	53	0.63
Green manuring	1.28	2.0	50.3	0.39	0.24	52	0.51

Organic farming promote and maintain higher productivity, provide greater stability in crop productions, correct secondary and micronutrient deficiencies and have beneficial influence on physical and biological properties of soil. Organic manures improves moisture content, soil structure build up and stability, maintain optimum air-water relationship. Retention and release of nutrients are favoured with organic. Organic manures are a valuable nutrient source, their regular addition enhances biological activity and diversity, improves soil tilth and water relations. Integrating inorganic with organic will go a long way in maintaining sustainable crop production and enhancing soil fertility through complementary effects.

References

Aggarwal, P., D.K. Parashar, Y. Kumar, and R.P. Gupta (1997) "Effect of Kharif green manuring and rabi tillage on physical properties of puddled clay loam under rice-wheat rotation." *Journal of Indian Society of Soil Science* 45: 434-437.

Bullakki, M.A. and V.P. Badanur (1994) "Effect of crop residue incorporation on physical and chemical properties of soil of a vertisol and yield of Sorghum." *Journal of Indian Society of Soil Science* 42: 533-535.

Bullakki M.A. and V.P. Badanur (1997) "Long-term effect of integrated nutrient management on properties of vertisol under dry land agriculture" *Journal of India Society of Soil Science* 45: 438-441.

Mathur, G.M. (1997) "Effect of long-term application of fertilizers and manures on soil properties and yield under Cotton-Wheat rotation in north-west Rajasthan." *Journal of Indian Society of Soil Science* 45 : 288-291.

Meelu, O.P. (1996) "Integrated nutrient management for ecological sustainable agriculture." *Journal of Indian Society of Soil Science* 44 : 582-592.

Nambiar, K.K.M. (1994) *Soil fertility and crop productivity under long-term fertilizer use in India* I.C.A.R. New Delhi.

Somani L.L., Totawat K.L. and Baser B.L. (1992) Proceedings of National Seminar on Natural Farming, Rajasthan Agricultural University, College of Agriculture, Udaipur.

Chapter 16

Protecting Soil Environment through Organic Farming

K.L. Totawat
Assoc. Prof., Ag. Chem. & Soil Science, RCA, Udaipur

There have been a long succession of changes in agriculture from nomadic harvest of natural products to the sophisticated cropping systems of present day agriculture. In modern agriculture a drastic change has occurred leading to rather a dynamic inorganic-dependent agriculture which was at some time a static-soil dependent. With the development of irrigation resources from 23 m ha to 89.4 m ha coupled with about 200 fold increase in fertilizer use (0.07 mt in 1950 to 14.3 mt in 1996-97) and a significant improvement in plant type through genetic engineering, India has increased its food-grain production from 50 mt (1950) to 198.2 mt (1996-97) in last five decades. Such revolution in agriculture has enabled the country to become self-sufficient in foodgrain production but at the cost of exploitation of natural resources.

Cycling of Plant Nutrients

At the congress on "Cycling of Mineral Nutrients in Agricultural Ecosystem" held at Amsterdam in 1976 it was stressed that the consumable N-output (*i.e.* production of nitrogen in foods and feeds) is positively correlated with the total farm input of nitrogen. Furthermore, a higher N-output is accompanied by a proportionately higher farm output of P and K. However, such relationship will depend on the nutrient supplying power of the soil. In case supply of these nutrients is not adequate, they have to be supplied in the form of fertilizers, organic manures or concentrated feeds. Kolenbrander (1982) has also reported a higher N-input can contribute to a higher output of consumable N accompanied with heavier loss of N, P and K from the soil to the environment. The greatest loss of N, P and K occurs in the form of food consumed by the population the excrements of which, for reasons of hygiene, are not conserved properly and scientifically.

Environmental Implications of Chemical Farming

Kolenbrander (1982) while describing the nitrogen cycle of an arable farm through a schematic representation has shown three "Leaks" in the cycle:

1. Export of food from the farm (N, P, K) to the population (consumable),
2. Leaching to ground water (N, P, K), and
3. Volatilisation to the atmosphere (N).

There exists a relationship between these "leaks" and N-input (Table 1) on arable farm a higher N-input though resulted in a higher consumable output of N, P and K but has increased the losses of nutrients through leaching and denitrification. The minerals in food consumed by the population will be excreted almost entirely and if not conserved, transported directly or indirectly with waste water to the ocean.

Table 1

Average Output of N, P and K as A Function of Total N-Input

N-Input kg N ha^{-1} yr^{-1}	*Type of Output*	*Output (Kg ha^{-1} yr^{-1})*			
		N	*%*	*K*	*P*
100	Consumable	70	(70)	70	11
100	Leached	10	(10)	13	Traces
100	Denitrify. + NH_3	20	(20)	-	-
200	Consumable	130	(65)	130	20
200	Leached	30	(15)	20	Traces
200	Denitrif. + NH_3	40	(21)	-	-
300	Consumable	180	(60)	180	28
300	Leached	66	(22)	43	Traces
300	Denitrif. + NH_3	51	(17)	-	-

Traces = 0-2 kg ha^{-1} yr^{-1}.

* Figures in parentheses indicate percentages of N-output.

Volatilisation Losses of N and Health Hezards

Loss of applied urea -N by volatilisation in typic ustochrept of IARI, New Delhi was 12-15 per cent under wheat-maize cropping system, whereas the same was 29 per cent in rice in Vertic Ustochrepts of Coimbatore (Anonymous, 1988). Van-Breeman *et al.,* (1982) have reported that volatilisation losses of ammonia is not only of concern from the viewpoint of plant nutrition but is back deposition on earth's surface induces acidification of soil. Ammonia in the atmosphere reacts with sulphate and/or oxides of sulphur, emanating mostly from industries, to yield ammonium sulphate which after deposition on earth's surface converts to acids as stated below:

$$(NH_4)_2SO_4 + 4O_2 \rightarrow 2HNO_3 + H_2SO_4 + 2H_2O$$

Denitrification, the biological reduction of nitrates or nitrites to gaseous form of the nitrogen either as molecular dinitrogen (N_2) or as oxide of nitrogen of applied nitrogenous fertilizers has potentials of emitting oxides of nitrogen into atmosphere. Whereas N_2 is environmentally enert, N_2O has implications as it has been linked with catalytic reduction of ozone in stratosphere, the reduction of later will increase the risk of incidences of skin cancer on earth as ozone layer protects the earth from UV radiations. However, it is fortunate that N_2O emission as compared to N_2 due to denitrification is relatively small and constitute significant proportion only when nitrate containing fertilizer are applied on acidic soils (Rolston, 1981).

Katyal (1989) calculated the current atmospheric burden of N_2O at 1500 Tg (Terragram) (1500 million tonnes) and showed that N_2O burden was increasing @ 0.2 per cent per annum; agricultural land contributed 0.8 Tg/annum. Further, with life time of 100-175 years nitrous oxide accumulation will assume alarming proportions.

Green House Gases and Global Warming

Environmental concern emanates from the fact that N_2O, CO_2 and CH_4 in the atmosphere with an increase in use of fertilizer in agriculture (Gushee, 1989 and Bouwman, 1990). The anthropogenic activities have already increased the concentrations of green house gases in the air contributing substantially to global warming (Table 2).

Table 2
Green House Gases Concentration

Gas	***Surface Air Concentration ppm (Volume) in Year***			***Recent Growth Per cent/Year***	***Expected Relative Contributions to Global Warming (%)***
	1600	***1800***	***1985***		
CO_2	280.00	280.00	345.00	0.2-0.5	47
CH_2	0.70	1.15	1.65	1.20	14
N_2O	0.28	0.28	0.30	0.2-0.3	10
CFCs	0.00	0.00	0.005	5.80	23

Nitrate Pollution

Accelerated use of nitrogenous fertilizers (present day trend in agriculture) has potential for increasing nitrous oxide emissions besides charging groundwater with nitrates.

Leaching of applied N depends upon amount of water percolating through the soil and the presence of excess nitrate-N in the soil. Although elevated use of nitrogenous fertilizer is the main source of nitrate but there are many other sources of nitrate-N such as sewage effluent, animal excreta, natural soil nitrate and decomposition of soil organic matter (Keeny, 1989). In many regions, natural deposits of nitrate may constitute a major source for nitrate pollution of ground water (Handa, 1987)(Table 3).

Table 3
Nitrate Content of Well Waters

District	***State***	***NO_3-N (mg/l)***
Aligarh	Utter Pradesh	61
Meerut	Utter Pradesh	157
Mahendragarh	Haryana	296
Ambala	Haryana	223
Bhatinda	Punjab	128
Sangrur	Punjab	98

World Health Organisation has recommended that ground water containing < 11.3 mg NO_3-N per litre is safe for drinking purposes. Elevated concentration of nitrates in drinking water, particularly when the later is contaminated with bacteria, have been associated with to cause blue baby disease (methaemoglobinaemia) in infant and babies. Carcinogenic nitrosamines by reaction of ingested amines with nitrite in the human stomach may present a further health hazard after exposure to high levels of nitrate. Data relating exposure to nitrate or nitrite to the incidence of cancer have also been reported (Fraser and Chilvers, 1981). Nitrate-N may also affect the cardiac functions of man.

Heavy Metal Pollution

Fertilizers contain heavy metals as impurities. Application of rock phosphate or its products to soil always implies the addition of a significant amount of lead and cadmium into the soil (Table 4) (Arora *et al.,* 1975; Bijay Singh and Sekhon, 1977; Tiller, 1989).

Table 4

Lead and Cadmium Content (mg/kg) of Fertilizers

Fertilizer	*Lead*		*Cadmium*
	(1)	*(2)*	*(1)*
Urea	-	4	1
Calcium ammonium nitrate	116	200	6
Muriate of potash	117	88	14
Diammonium phosphate	195	188	109
Super phosphate	487	609	187
Rock phosphate	962	1135	303

* (1) Arora *et al.*, 1975.
(2) Bijay Singh & Sekhon, 1977.

Data available suggest that heavy metals applied to the soil through different derivation of rock phosphate accumulate almost completely in the surface layer of the soil in forms generally easily available to plants (Williams and David, 1973). In course textured soils with low pH availability of heavy metals applied through fertilizers was more as compared to soil containing large amount of clay and with alkaline reaction (Mortvedt and Osborn, 1982; Rana and Kansal, 1983).

Nutrient Imbalance and Crop Productivity

With almost twice the quantity of plant nutrients being removed from soil than what is added through fertilizers. The growing nutrient imbalance poses a serious threat to sustain soil health and crop productivity. Further, the present day inorganic (fertilizer) dependent farming is encountering serious problems like:

I. Surface heardening,
II. Compaction by tillage emplements,
III. Proneness to erosion,
IV. Low fertility,
V. Shallow depth etc.

and is not in a position to sustain the productivity. Intensive tillage used for loosening crusted soil and enhanced infiltration also resulted in increased rate of decomposition of organic matter.

Under such circumstances along with environmental implications use of inorganics (Chemical fertilizers) alone is not a sound practice. All these facts call for to substitute the fertilizer by organics. Organic farming envisage the use of organic manures, crop wastes biological nitrogen, use of bio-fertilizers, legume in crop rotation, green manuring etc.

Potential Organic Resources

Livestock and Human Wastes

Animal Excreta

Rajasthan has good potential for recycling animal excreta through manuring. Data presented in Table 5 clearly indicate that the gross availability of animal excreta to be more than 100 million tonnes per year.

Table 5

Potential Availability of Animal Excreta in Rajasthan

Animal	*Population (thousand)*	*Average Dung/Animal (t/yr)*	*Gross Dung Available mt*
Cattle	11322	3.5	39.63
Buffalo	7747	5.0	38.74
Sheep and Goat	28031	0.7	19.62
Camel	739	7.0	5.17
Poultry	2993	0.006	0.02
Total			103.18

Almost 21.2 per cent of this dung is used as fueld cakes (Sinha and Kishore, 1989). As such 81.33 million tonnes of dung is left available for recycling in soil. On the basis of 75 per cent moisture the dry matter available is 20.3 million tonnes/year. This dry matter contain 1.5 per cent N, 1.0 per cent P_2O_5 and 0.8 per cent K_2O, providing 0.3, 0.2 and 0.16 million tonnes per year of N, P_2O_5 and K_2O respectively. The total cultivable area (net sown area) of the state is 16.12 million hectare, the contribution of N, P_2O_5 and K_2O per hectare through animal excreta recycling would be 18.6, 12.4 and 9.9 kg/ha respectively.

There is a vast scope to establish biogas plants which can save dung being wasted in fuel cakes and total recyclable nutrients could be increased 20 per cent over the figures computed as above. Establishment of biogas plants will also conserve the animal urine which is richer part of animal excreta and thus will further increase the quantity of recyclable nutrients from animal yard.

The annual out-turn of animal urine from different groups of cattle and buffalow from Rajasthan comes out to be 53.31 million tonnes, carrying 0.1, 0.005 and 0.1 million tonne/year of N, P_2O_5 and K_2O.

Human Waste

The present human population is reaching to a count 1000 million mark. The daily excretion per head averaged out to be 0.133 kg of solid waste and 1.21 of urine. The data computed on annual basis will come out to be 46.12 million tonnes of faeces and 438 million tonnes of urine. The manurial potential of human excreta approximately comes out to be 5.1, 1.2 and 1.1 million tonnes of N, P_2O_5 and K_2O respectively.

Since night soil (human waste) is an important bulky organic manure supplying a good deal of organic matter and plant nutrients to the soil, its proper conservation and recycling is a must to harness its beneficial values in organic farming.

Slaughter House Wastes

There are about 3,000 slaughter houses in the country handling annually 40 million sheep and goats and 1.5 million buffaloes (Gaur *et al.,* 1984). About 12 million dead large animals are available annually. No systematic steps are taken towards organised collection of bones from dead animals and their utilisation. It is estimated that about 4.5 lakh tonnes of bones are available every year of which only 1.36 lakh tonnes are collected and utilised by bone crushing mills. Bone meal contains about 1 to 2 per cent nitrogen besides 25 to 30 per cent P_2O_5. Enormous amount of nitrogen and phosphorous can be supplied by proper utilisation of bonemeal potential.

Apart from bonemeal nearly 5,000 tonnes of leather wastes can be collected from slaughtered and fallen animals for use of organic fertilizer which remains unutilised at present.

Crop Residue and Aquatic Weeds

Crop Wastes

Huge quantity of renewable crop residues produced every year in the country (Table 6). Major cereal crops alone yield approximately 141.2 million tonnes of straw and about 10 million tonnes of legume residues are at our disposal. Cereal straw and residues on maturity contain 0.5, 0.6 and 1.5 per cent N, P_2O_5 and , K_2O respectively. The quantity of nutrients in legume residues is much higher than in cereal straw. The nutrient potential of cereal residues worked out to be 0.7, 0.84 and 2.1 million tonnes of N, P_2O_5 and K_2O per annum. Even if 50 per cent of these crop residues are utilised as animal feed, the rest, if mobilised for recycling can serve a good source of plant nutrient apart from having other beneficial effect on soil properties.

Table 6
Potential of Crop Residues for Recycling

Crop	***Average Grain: Straw Ratio***	***Area ('000 ha)***	***Average Yield (kg ha^{-1})***	***Production ('000 tonnes)***	***Dry Matter Yield ('000 tonnes)***
Paddy	(1:1.02)	39688	1246	74474.2	89,369.04
Sorghum	(1:1.50)	16101	592	9525.0	14,287.50
Wheat	(1:0.65)	20112	1409	28336.0	18,418.40
Bajra	(1:1.50)	11583	494	5726.0	8,589.00
Maize	(1:1.50)	5996	1173	7036.0	19,554.00
Total cereals		103,522	1040	107,698.0	-
Total pulses	(1:0.75)	24665	533	13,135.0	9,851.25

Aquatic Weeds-Water Hyacinth

Water hyacinth (*Eichhornia crassipes*) is a free floating weed plant which grows luxuriantly in ponds, lakes and water reservoir. It is estimated that total acreage under this weed is about 292,000 ha in Bengal, Bihar, Assam, Eastern UP, Andhra Pradesh, Tamil Nadu, Orissa and Kerala (Gaur, *et al.,* 1984). Even in northern part of the country it is flourishing in most of the water reservoirs. It can be used as soil mulch, greenmanure as well as to prepare compost. Attempts have also been made to use water hyacinth for biogas production without loss of plant nutrients. It has potential to yield about 250 tonnes ha^{-1} $year^{-1}$ and thus there is a potential for producing 3 million tonnes of compost annually containing plant nutrients to the extent of 20.5 kg N, 11.0 kg P_2O_5 and 25 kg K_2O per tonne.

Green Manuring

Green Manuring in Situ

In this system green manure crops are grown and buried in the same field after 8 weeks of growth to improve soil fertility of raising another crop. The most common green manure crops grown are sannhemp (*Crotularia juncea*), dhaincha (*Sesbania aculeata*), pillipesara (*Phaseulas trilobus*) and guar (*Cyamopsis tetragonaloba*) etc. This system is more common in northern India, but the practice is becoming uncommon in the recent past.

Green Leaf Manuring

Green leaf manuring refers to turning into the soil green leaves and tender green twings collected from shrubs and trees grown on bunds, wastelands and nearby forest areas. The common shrubs and trees used are Glyricidia (*Glyricida maculata*), *Sesbania speciosa*, Karanj (*Pongamia pinnata*) etc. This system is more common in eastern, southern and central India.

There is a need to develop a programme for raising wild legumes on bunds and wastelands for increasing the scope of green leaf manuring to advocate its adoption without loosing a crop.

Rural and Urban Wastes

The rural and urban wastes available are if properly conserved and diverted for rural and town compost will not only generate a good source of organic matter but will also create a hygienic condition and a step ahead to reduce environmental pollution. There is a need to set up mechanised plants in the town areas to improve the efficiency of the present day effort. Gaur *et al.* (1984) have reported the available potentiality of rural and town compost to the extent of 600 million and 15 million tonnes, respectively. The urban population mostly linked with drainage system produces a hung quantity of sewage annually which can be diverted after proper treatment for sewage irrigation. Such an effort will not only provide water, plant nutrients and organic matter for crop, production will also be an effective method to protect our environment.

References

Anonymous, 1988. *Progress of research work, Indo-US SSP programme in agriculture*, ICAR & DST, New Delhi.

Arora, C.L.; Nayyar, V.K. and Randhawa, N.S., 1975. "Note on secondary and microelement contents of fertilizers and manures." *Indian J. Agric. Sci.* 45: 80-85.

Bijay Singh and Sekhon, G.S., 1979. "Impact of fertilizer use on environmental pollution in Punjab - present status and future projections." *Fert. News* 23(2): 7-11.

Bouman, A.F., 1990. *Soils and green house effect*, Wiley, Chichester.

Fraser, P. And Chilvers, C., 1981. "Health aspects of nitrate in drinking water." *Sci. Total Envir.* 18: 103-116.

Gaur, A.C.; Neelakantan, S. and Dargan, K.S., 1984. *Organic manures*, ICAR, New Delhi, p 159.

Gushee, D.E., 1989. *Chemtech* 19(8): 470-479.

Handa, B.K., 1987. "Nitrate content of ground water in India." *Fert. News*. 32: 11-29.

Katyal, J.C., 1989. Proc. FAI Annual seminar pp S VI/2-1-1-S VI/2-8.

Keeney, D.R., 1989. "Sources of nitrate to ground water." In : R.F. Follet, (ed)., *Nitrogen management and ground water protection.* Elsevier Amsterdam, pp 23-34.

Kolenbrander, G.J., 1982. "Fertilizers and pollution., Whither soil research Trans." *12Th Int. Congr. Soil Sci.* 248-266.

Mortvedt, J.J. and Osborn, G., 1982. "Studies on the chemical from of cadmium contaminants in phosphatic fertilizers." *Soil Sci.* 134: 185-192.

Rana, R.L. and Kansal, B.D., 1983. "Sorption an drelease of cadmium in sewage irrigation soils." *J. Indian Soc. Soil Sci.* 31: 439-443.

Rolston, D.E., 1981. In: Delwiche, C.C. (ed), *Denitrification, nitrofication, atmospheric nitrous oxide*, pp 127-149, 241-277. John Wiley and Sons, New York, USA.

Sinha, C.S. and Kishore, V.V.N., 1989. "Potential for biogas in Rajasthan." In: *Renewable Energy for rural development*. Tata McGraw-Hill, New Delhi, pp 536-540.

Tiller, K.G., 1989. *Heavy metals in soils and their environmental significance*. Aust. Soils Div. Rep. No. 13.

Van Breeman, N.; Burrough, P.A.; Velthorst, E.A.J.; Van-Dobben, H.F.; Toka De Wit; Ridder, T.R. and Rejnders, H.F.R., 1982. *Nature*, 299: 594-550.

Williams, C.H. and David, D.J., 1973. "The effect of superphosphate on the cadmium content of soils plants." *Aust. J. Soil Res.* 11: 43-56.

Chapter 17

Rhizobium: A Bio-Fertilizer for Legumes

K.L. Totawat

Assoc. Prof., Dept. of Ag. Chem. & Soil Sc., RCA, Udaipur

The major nutrient input in crop cultivation is nitrogen. It is freely available in the atmosphere but has to be fixed in the form to be made use as a plant nutrient. Chemical fixation as ammonia by way of combining elemental nitrogen and hydrogen is highly expensive. Fertilizer is one of the most effective but expensive farm input in crop production. The nitrogen fertilizer requirements for crop production by 2000 A.D. is estimated to be about 11.4×10^6 tonnes as against 8.59×10^6 tonnes at present (1996-97). There is a vast gap which cannot be filled up merely through the production of synthetic nitrogenous fertilizers. Biological fixation of nitrogen from the atmosphere through free-living micro-organism and plant micro-organism associations with the help of enzyme nitrogenase is the key to sustain agricultural production at low cost involvement without depleting fossil fuel. Our atmosphere has nearly three-fourth nitrogen (77% by volume) and it is estimated that above each hectare of land there are about 80,000 tonnes of nitrogen available in atmosphere. But atmospheric nitrogen is not available to plants or animals and they cannot make use of free nitrogen. Plant starve and crop productivity is limited by this element.

Atmospheric Nitrogen Fixation

Nitrogen fixation by micro-organisms (Table 1) has been going on in the biosphere ever since land plants established symbiotic or near symbiotic relationships with plants. The role of legumes in enriching the fertility of soil was known through centuries, however, scientific demonstration of the value of legumes in contributing to the nitrogen nutrition of plants were only done in first half of twentieth century (Fred *et al.* 1932). It was first time conclusively established that nodule on legume roots are responsible for fixing atmospheric nitrogen through the bacterium *Rhizobium*. Our present knowledge about biochemistry, physiology and genetic regulation of the biological nitrogen fixation along with the newer technological developments can make a substantial contribution in increasing production of legumes besides improving the N-fertility of cultivated soils.

Table 1
Important Micro-Organisms Contributing Nitrogen Nutrition to Plants

Micro-Organisms	***Nitrogen Fixed ($kg\ N\ ha^{-1}\ year^{-1}$)***
Actinorrhizae *(Frankia* sp.*)*	150
Azospirillum	10-20
Azotobacter	0.026-20
Rhizobium	50-300
Azolla	900
Algae	25

Source: Shroff (1992)

What is A Bio-Fertilizer?

Bio-fertilizers are microbial inoculant have attended a special significance in modern agriculture. It is a living fertilizer composed of microbial inoculant or groups of micro-organisms, known as biological nitrogen fixers. They can be grouped into three major categories:

a. Free living bacteria (Azotobacter and Azospirillum)
b. The blue green algae
c. Symbionts such as Rhizobium

Legumes as Nitrogen Fixer

Legumes play unique role in plant kingdom and rank third amongst flowering plants in number of species they contain. Most of the species are trees, shrubs and wood vines. The cultivated species includes mainly food, forage any pasture plants. Of the 1,300 species examined, representing all the three sub-families of Leguminosae about 14 per cent were found to be non-nodulating (Allen and Allen, 1961). Among different legumes examined in Indian soils, except the species of *Cassia* and *Glcine max,* all nodulate well although they vary in extent of nodulation (Rangaswamy and Oblisamy, 1962; Satyanarayana and Gaur, 1965; Sundara Rao *et al.,* 1972). Date (1970) reported that a symbiotic fixation of 10 kg nitrogen is equivalent to an application of 50 kg of ammonium sulphate, however, symbiotically fixed nitrogen is in organic form, there would be little loss and therefore would be equivalent to an effective application of 100 kg of ammonium sulphate.

Rhizobium Bio-Fertilizer

Rhizobium bio-fertilizer is the best known bio-fertilizer. Rhizobium fixes atmospheric nitrogen symbiotically with legumes. Legumes can obtain their nitrogen from the atmosphere via the activity of N_2 fixing bacteria of the genus *Rhizobium* located is swelling on the roots called nodules. This symbiosis is extremely important in agriculture when legumes are grown for food and its responsible for major input for the nitrogen cycle on a global scale. The amount of nitrogen fixed every year varies from 50 to 300 kg per hectare, thus, saving a considerable quantity of money of our poor peasant which they would otherwise have to spend on nitrogen fertilizers.

Rhizobium is abundant in soil and all of them are not able to nodulate all types legumes. Seven host or cross inoculation groups are recognised on the basis of ability of rhizobia to form nodules with legumes (Table 2). However, Rhizobium is not entirely restricted to leguminous hosts only. This is also capable of nodulating the non-legume *Parasponia* belonging to the family Ulmaceae.

Table 2
Classification of Rhizobium

Group	Rhizobium	Legume Host
Fast Growing Species		
I.	*R. leguminosarum*	Pea, Broad bean, Vetch, Lentil
II.	*R. phaseoil*	Runner bean, Kidney bean
III.	*R. trifoli*	Clover
IV.	*R. meliloti*	Alfalfa
Slow Growing Species		
V.	*R. japonicum*	Soybean
VI.	*R. lupini*	Lupin
VII.	*Rhizobium* spp. (miscellany)	Cowpea, peanut

Rhizobia have been divided into two groups based on their growth habits (Table 2). One is fast grower producing acid on the yeast-mannitol-agar and the other is slow-growing strain producing alkali on yeast-mannitol-agar.

Infection and Nodulation

Rhizobium multiplies rapidly in the legume rhizosphere and the distribution along the root is uneven. It is difficult to determine how many rhizobia are needed for infection and nodulation. As few as 10-15 rhizobia on the seed, which later multiply may be sufficient for maximum nodulation. A large population of nodulating rhizobia promotes early infection and nodulation.

Attachment and Curling of Root Hair

The accumulation and subsequent polar attachment of Rhizobium to legume root is the first step leading to infection and nodulation. Rhizobia enter the roots of legumes either through root hair or directly at the point of emergence of lateral roots. Thr root cap cells and probably also the epidermal cells secrete large amounts of polysaccharide (Bell and McCully, 1970) and globules of material may also form at root hair tips (Head, 1964). This material forms the "mucigel," a coating of variable thickness along the young roots which often extends beyond the root hair. Curling or controlled growth and branching of root hair is the firstly visible plant response to *Rhizobium* (Nutman, 1959). Curling of root hair is caused by secretion of the bacteria, *i.e.* the production of IAA (indole acetic acid) in the rhizosphere of legumes.

Formation of Infection Thread and Its Growth

Nutman (1958) suggested that for infection process no actual penetration of the bacterium into the root hair is required. The root hair cell-wall becomes invaginated to form the infection thread. The infection thread penetrates through the cortex and comes in contact with a preformed tetraploid cells which forms a 'unit' with the surrounding diploid cells. The unit undergoes maristematic division to form the young nodule. The diploid cells constitute the apical meristem of the developing nodule and remain relatively free of the ramifications of the branches of the infection thread, while the tetraploid cells soon get traversed by the branches of the original infection thread to constitute the central infected zones.

A mature nodule consists of a central "bacteriod zone" containing bacteroids which is surrounded by the nodule cortex. The bacteroids are enclosed in membrane envelopes of host origin. Bacteriods are normally nonmotile. The volume and number of bacteriods have a direct relationship with the nitrogen fixation.

With the formation of bacteriods a red pigment haemoglobin accumulates between the bacteriods and the membermous envelopes. This pigment is known as "leghaemoglobin", the prefix leg indicating its presence in leguminous rot nodule. Leghaemoglobin is only present in infected cells and its location is confined to the host cytoplasm (Verma and Bal, 1976). The amount of leghaemoglobin and bacteroid production had direct relationship with amount of N_2 fixed by legumes (Chopra and Suba Rao, 1967; Tilak and Saxena, 1976).

Factors Affecting Symbiosis and Nitrogen Fixation by Legume

Host Genotype

There is a marked effect of genetic character of the host plant on the results of symbiosis (Parker, 1957 and Nutman, 1959). Tilak (1991) has reported that plants which were sensitive to nodulation had high C:N ratio.

Effectiveness of Rhizobial Strains

Most of the soils contain rhizobia which range in effectiveness from highly beneficial strains to those of little or no value. Several studies have shown that host plant is the dominant factor in assessing the effective and ineffective strains of rhizobia (Burton, 1952, 1964; Burton *et al.* 1954). Results of different studies have indicated that some strains of rhizobia are more acceptable than others to a particular host plant. It is still undecided that the property of nodulation should be attributed to rhizobia, to the host or to both of the symbionts. The plants nodulated by ineffective ryizobial strain showed lower dry-matter yield, grain yield and nitrogen content irrespective of number of nodules than the effective strains of Rhizobium.

Effect of Other Micro-Organisms in Rhizosphere

There may be variation is nitrogen fixation efficiency of rhizobia tested in green house and under field conditions. One of the factors responsible for this variation in ability of rhizobial strains is the presence of antagonistic microflora (Burton, 1964). The aerobic spore forming bacteria and the streptomycetes are the most active antagonists to the rhizobia (Allen and Allen, 1961). In general, the slow-growing rhizobia appear to be the most susceptible to the actionmycetes (Abdel-Ghaffar and Allen, 1950).

Organic Matter

The presence of organic matter in soil had a favourable influence on the number of rhizobia. Iswaran *et al.* (1979) and Singh and Tilak (1977) have reported heavy nodulation of certain pulses in soil enriched with charcoal. However, others have reported that addition of activated vermiculite or phosphorus and potassium fertilizers are better than any of the organic materials. On the other hand Dev and Tilak (1976) have reported the FYM proved better than organic cakes like neem - cake, mahua cake, and alsicake for nodulation of legumes.

Temperature

Root temperature has marked effect on the efficiency of rhizobia (Gibson, 1967). The nitrogen level in the roots of nodulated plants is a function of strain of *Rhizobium* used. However, the distribution of nitrogen between roots and shoots is controlled by the effect of root temperature. Effective symbiosis is also hampered sometimes at high temperatures (Burton, 1964).

Sunlight and Drying

Rhizobia die quickly under drying conditions, the rate of death is influenced by type of inoculum and age of culture. Cells of freshly inoculated culture do not withstand drying as much as the physiologically old culture.

Nutritional Factor

Application of mineral nitrogen to legume may inhibit nitrogen fixation depending upon the kind of plant and the form in which nitrogen is applied. High doses of nitrogenous fertilizers decreased the nitrogen fixation, whereas lower dose increased the symbiosis and growth of legume. P, K, Ca and Mg are other elements affecting the symbiotic relationship. Calcium is highly essential for the growth of rhizobia. The rhizobial cell has a specific requirement for calcium or magnesium. Cobalt is another important growth factor for rhizobia *in vitro*. Likewise, molybdenum plays an important role in the transfer of electrons. Elements like iron, copper and cobalt have been involved in leghaemoglobin synthesis (Burris, 1966).

Method of Application of Rhizobium Inoculants

Carrier based cultures are suspended in 10 per cent sugar or gur (Jaggery) solution in water. The sugar or gur solution is boiled and cooled before the culture is sprinkled on the seeds and the seeds are thoroughly mixed so as to have uniform coating. A count of 1,000 viable cells per seed is to be attained at the time of treating the seed and the quantity of culture used to be accordingly adjusted. Usually, 400 g of peat, lignite, or charcoal based culture or 900 g soil based culture would be sufficient to the quantity of seed required per hectare.

Field Responses of Pulses to Rhizobium Inoculation

All India Coordinated Pulse Improvement Research Project (ICAR) have shown the substantial yield improvement as a result of rhizobial inoculation. There was a marked improvement in the yield of legume crops over uninoculated control (Table 3) (Rewari, 1984, 1985).

Table 3

Response of Different Pulse Crops to Inoculation with Rhizobial Cultures under Different Agro-Climatic Conditions

Crop	Location	Range of Per cent Increase in Grain Yield of Different Cultivars Treated with Various Rhizobial Cultures over Uninoculated Control
Mungbean	Lam, Andhra Pradesh,	1.4-75.0
	Dholi, Bihar	16.00-49.0
	Delhi	13.0-33.0
	Pantnagar, Uttar Pradesh	4.0-15
Urdbean	Pudukkonai, Tamil Nadu	4.0-21.0
	Dholi, Bihar	11.0-29.0
	Pantnagar, Uttar Pradesh	17.0-21.0
Cowpea	Sardar Krishi Nagar, Gujarat	1.0-36.0
	Coimbatore, Tamil Nadu	No response
Pigeonpea	Hissar, Haryana	5.0-25.0
	Pantnagar, Utter Pradesh	2.0-25.0
	S.K. Nagar, Gujarat	9.0-21.0
	Sehore, Madhya Pradesh	13.0-29.0
	Rahuri, Maharashtra	3.0-40.0
Chickpea	Varanasi, Uttar Pradesh	4.0-19.0
	Dholi, Bihar	25.0-42.0
	Delhi	18.0-28.0
	Hissar, Haryana	24.0-43.0
	Dohad, Gujarat	33.0-67.0
	Sehore, Madhya Pradesh	20.0-21.0
	ICRISAT, Hyderabad	No response
	Badnapur, Maharashtra	8.0-12.0
Lentil	Pantangar, Uttar Pradesh	4.0-26.0
	Ludhiana, Punjab	No response

Source: Rewari, 1984, 1985.

The present increase in yield due to *Rhizobium* inoculation varied from 16-65, 6-64, 20-63 and 14-41 over uninoculated controls in case of pegionpea, childpea, lentil and cowpea, respectively (Subba Rao and Tilak, 1984). Rhizobial culture have been tested in farmers field (Table 4) and found to be beneficial.

Table 4

Response of Different Pulses to Rhizobial Inoculation at Farmers' Fields

Crop	***Location***		***Grain Yield (q/ha)***		***Increase Over Control***	
			Control	***Inoculated***	***q/ha***	***Percent***
Urdbean	Bangalore Karnataka	1.	12.05	14.20	2.15	18
		2.	7.75	9.00	1.25	16
		3.	7.25	8.25	1.00	14
		4.	8.25	10.50	2.25	27
		5.	6.75	6.75	-	-
	Lam, A.P	No response to inoculation				
Cow pea	Bangalore Karnataka	1.	10.30	12.50	2.20	21
		2.	9.0	10.05	1.05	12
Pigeonpea	Gulburga, Karnataka	1.	18.50	19.85	1.35	7
	Sehore, M.P.	1.	5.10	5.92	0.82	16
		2.	4.95	5.89	0.94	19
Mungbean	Lam, A.P.	No response to inoculation				
Lentil	Dholi Bihar	1.	19.00	20.00	1.00	5
		2.	13.50	15.75	2.25	17
		3.	17.00	18.25	1.25	7
Chckpea	Badnapur, Maharashtra	1.	9.25	10.85	1.60	17
		2.	9.00	10.45	1.45	16
		3.	8.95	11.05	2.10	23
		4.	10.20	10.90	0.70	7
		5.	8.85	10.55	1.70	19
		6.	8.45	10.00	1.55	18

Crop	Location		Grain Yield (q/ha)		Increase Over Control	
			Control	Inoculated	q/ha	Percent
	Hissar, Haryana	1.	7.60	9.30	1.70	22
		2.	5.50	6.00	0.50	6
		3.	14.00	16.00	2.00	14
		4.	10.40	10.44	0.04	-
		5.	13.20	14.00	0.80	6
		6.	6.00	6.10	0.10	-
		7.	13.10	13.42	0.32	2
		8.	12.00	12.20	0.20	2
		9.	14.25	15.05	0.80	6
		10.	10.07	10.35	0.28	3
		11.	10.95	11.43	0.48	4
	Berhampore, W. Bengal	1.	4.45	7.34	2.89	65
		2.	6.38	6.47	0.09	-

Source: Rewari, 1984, 1985.

Cereal-Legume Association: Effect on Companion and Succeeding Cereals

The main advantages of legume-non legume, association are better utilisation of environmental resources, improved nutrient recycling, building up of soil nitrogen status and increase in N-available to the companion non-legume and ultimately the net return and sometimes the quality of the non-legume (Patra, 1990). Nitrogen fixed by a legume may concurrently be available to the associated non-legume either through root exudates or through decay of nodules. The effect of N fixed by a legume is also carried over to the succeeding crops (De 1982). Inter-cropping increased maize yields by 10.3, 16.42, 16.82 and 68 per cent with cow pea, moongbean, groundnut and *phaseolus vulgaris,* respectively (Gunasena and Sangakkara 1979).

Patra *et al.* (1990) observed a higher per cent N content in wheat (grain) grown after cowpea as sole or intercrop. Both dry matter yield and total N uptake was higher in wheat grown after sole or intercropped cow pea as compared to sole crop maize (Table 5).

Table 5
Effect of Maize-Cow Pea Inter Cropping on Succeeding Wheat

Previous Cropping	***% N in Wheat Grain***	***Total Dry Matter Yield q ha^{-1}***	***Total N Uptake kg ha^{-1}***
Maize sole crop	1.82	78.7	72.1
Maize + cowpea	1.93	84.9	89.6
Cowpea sole crop	2.03	91.4	101.4
CD (P=0.01)	0.12	4.01	3.48

Conclusion

Rhizobium is a key bacteria in biological nitrogen fixation to sustain agricultural productivity. Rhizobium inoculation of legume is very effective in harnessing atmospheric nitrogen for improving the nitrogen status of soils. The quantity of nitrogen fixed symbiotic varies from 50 to 300 kg ha^{-1} year^{-1}. The nitrogen fixed symbiotically not only benefits the host but also has a residual effect to benefit the subsequent crop.

References

Abdel-Gaffar, A.S. and Allen, O.N. 1950. "The effects of certain micro-organisms on the growth and function of rhizobia." Transactions of International Congress of Soil Science, 4th Congress, Amsterdam III, 3: 193.

Allen, E.K. and Allen, O.N. 1961. "Nitrogen fixation : The scope of nodulation in leguminaseae." In: *Recent Advances in Botany. Proceedings of 9th International Botanical Congress, Montreal,* 1959, Vol. 1 pp 586-88. University of Toronto Press, Canda.

Bell, J.K and McCully, M.E. 1970. *Protoplasma* 70: 179.

Burris, R.H. 1966. "Biological nitrogen fixation," *Annual Review of Plant Physiology* 17: 155-179.

Burton, J.C. 1952. "Host specificity among certain plants with cowpea cross-inoculation group." *Soil Science Soc. of America Proceedings* 16 : 356-58.

Burton, J.C. 1964. "The *Rhizobium* legume association. Microbiology and soil fertility." Preceedings of 194 Biology Colloquiam Cregon State press, Corvallis, pp 107-134.

Burton, J.C.; Allen, O.N. and Berger, K.C. 1954. "Response of beans (*Phaseolus valgaris* L.) to inoculation with mixtures of effective and ineffective rhizobia." *Soil Science Soc. of America Proceeding* 18 : 156-9.

Chopra, C.L. and Subba Rao, N.S. 1967. "Mutual relationship among bacterioids, leghaemoglobin and nitrogen content of Egyptian clover (*Trifolium alexanderium*) and gram (*Cicer arietinum*)" *Archieves of Microbiology* 58: 71-76.

Date, R.A. 1970. "Microbiology problem in the inoculation and nodualation of legumes." *Plant and Soil* 32: 702-25.

De, R. 1982. "Role of legumes in inter and sequential cropping systems in increasing soil productivity." Voluntary paper 12th Int. Congress Soil Sci. New Delhi, India, Feb. 8-16, 1982.

Dev, S.P. and Tilak K.V.B.R. 1976. "Effect of organic amendments on nodulation and nitrogen fixation by soybean." *Indian Journal of General Microbiology* 41: 85-91.

Fred, E.B.; Baldwin, I.L. and McCoy, E. 1932. *Root nodule bacteria and leguminous plants*. University of Wisconsin Press, Madison, U.S.A.

Gunasena, H.P.M. and Sangakkra, R. 1979. "Studies on cereal-legume intercropping system." *J. National Sci. Council*, 7(2) : 85:93.

Head, G.C. 1964. *Ann. Botany (London)* 28: 245.

Iswaran, V.; Bhatnagar, R.S., Jauhri, K.S. and Sen, A. 1979. "A comparative study of different carriers for *rhizobium* inoculants." *Indian J. Microbiology* 19 : 83-84.

Nutman, P.S. 1958. "The physiology of nodule formation." pp 87-106. In: *Nutrition of Legumes* (Ed.) Hallsworth, E.G. Buter Worths, London.

Nutman, P.S. 1959. "Some observations on root hair infection by nodule bacteria." *J. Environ. Botany* 10: 250-69.

Parker, C.A. 1957. "Evolution of nitrogen fixing symbiosis in higher plants." *Nature*, London 179: 593-94.

Patra, D.D. 1990. "Cereal-Legume Association - Effect on Companion and succeeding cereals." In : *Bio-fertilizer* (Ed.) Somani *et al.* Scientific Publishers, Jodhpur, India.

Patra, D.D.; Sachdev, M.S. and Subbiah, B.V. 1990. "Residual effect of cereal-legume intercropping on the N-availability of wheat from soils and fertilizer." In : *Bio-fertilizers* (Ed. Somani *et al.,* 1990). Scientific Publishers, Jodhpur, India 113-136.

Rangaswamy, G. and Oblisami, G. 1962. "Studies on some legume root nodule bacteria." *J. Indian Soc. Soil Science* 10:175-86.

Rewari, R.B. 1984. *Summarised results of microbiology trials.* All India Coordinated Research Project on Improvement of pulses, New Delhi, India

Rewari, R.B. 1985. *Summarised results of microbiology trials.* All India Coordinated Research Project on Improvement of Pulses, New Delhi, India.

Satyanarayana, Y. and Gaur, Y.D. 1965. "Preliminary studies on the nodulation of arid zone legumes." *Current Science* 34: 21-22.

Shroff, V.N. 1992. "Role of bio-fertilizers in crop production in Indian agriculture." In: *Bio-fertilizer Technology Transfer* (Gangawane, L.V.Ed.) Associated Publishing Company, New Delhi pp 12-20.

Singh, H.P. and Tilak, K.V.B.R. 1977. "Response of low-grade coal based inoculants of *Rhizobium janponicum* on the performance of soybean." *Indian J. Agron.* 22(1): 59-61.

Subba Rao, N.S. and Tilak, K.V.B.R. 1984. In: *Pulse Production-Constraints and Opportunities.* Oxford & IBH Publishing Co., New Delhi, pp 331-340.

Sundara Rao, W.V.B.; Sen, A.N. and Gaur, Y.D. 1972. *Survey and isolation of root nodule bacteria in Indian Soils.* Final Report of PL-480 Scheme, Division of Microbiology, IARI, New Delhi.

Tilak, K.V.B.R. 1991. *Bacterial fertilizers.* ICAR, New Delhi pp 66.

Tilak, KV.B.R. and Saxena, M.C. 1976. "Performance of peat-based single strains of *Rhizobium japonicum* on soyabean (*Glycine max*)." Proceedings of Indian National Science Academy 40(B) : 476-80.

Verma, D.P.S. and Bal, A.K. 1976. "Intracellar site of synthesis and localisation of leghaemoglobin in souybean root nodules." Proceedings of National Academy of Science, USA 23: 384-47.

Chapter 18

Azotobactor and *Azospirillum*: Bio-Fertilizers for Non-Legumes

A.K. Vyas

Deptt. of Agronomy, RCA, Udaipur

Some of soil micro-organisms play an important role in improving soil fertility and crop productivity due to thus capability to fix atmospheric nitrogen, solubilising insoluble phosphate and decompose farm nustes resulting in the release of plant nutrients. The extent of benefit from these micro-organisms depends upon their number and efficiency which is governed by a large number of soil and environmental factors. When the number and activity of specific micro-organism is sub-optimal, artificially multiplied culture of that micro-organism called microbial inoculant or bio-fertilizer is used to hasten biological activity to improve availability of plant nutrient.

Atmospheric nitrogen is fixed into the soil symbiotically by *Rhizobium* in legumes and asymbiotically by many micro-organisms mainly by *Azotobacter* and *Azospirillum* in non-legumes.

Azotobacter Inoculant

Based on morphological and physiological features, the genus *Azotobacter* has been classified in three species *i.e. Azotobacter chroococcum, A. Beijerinckii* and *A. vinelandii.* The first two species are most commonly occurring species in India. *Azotobacter chroococcum* appeared in acid soils while *A. beijerinckii* in neutral and alkali soils.

Beneficial Effect of Azotobacter

Azotobacter not only provides the N but produce a variety of growth promoting substances like indote acetic acid (IAA), gibberellins, B-vitamins and anti-fungal substances (Rao, 1975). *Azotobacter* has ability to produce anti-fungal antibiotics and fungistatic compounds against pathogens like *Fusarium, Alternaria, Trichoderma* (Lakshmi Kumari *et al.,* 1972). Mishustin and Naumowa (1962) found better development of shoot from *Azotobacter* culture treated seeds than control. Thus there was increased germination and vigour of young plants. Banerjee (1976) and Shendi *et al.* (1977) reported enhanced seed germination dut to *Azotobacter* inoculation. The onset of flowering of wheat was hastened (Rovira, 1965).

Another important characteristic of *Azotobacter* associated with crop improvement is excretion of ammonia in the rhizosphere in the presence of root exudates and helps in modification of nutrient uptake by the plant. Iswaran and Marwaha (1981) reported solubilisation different inorganic phosphates by *A. Chroococcum.*

Crop Response

The benefits of *Azotobacter* inoculation on crop production are well known. Crop receiving *Azotobacter* inoculation along with moderate levels of fertilizer N gave similar grain yields as the crop receiving higher doses of mineral fertilizers but uninoculated. This indicated the possibility of reducing fertilizer N application by inoculating the crop with appropriate strain (Wani, 1990).

The results from a large number of experiments conducted in last four decades have shown a positive response to *Azotobacter* application on a wide range of crops like cereals, millets, vegetables, cotton, sugarcane, etc. *Azotobacter* inoculation increased the crop yields by 0-30 per cent (Table 1). The beneficial effect is attributed to N_2-fixing capacity and also the ability to produce growth promoting substances.

Table 1
Effect of Azotobacter Inoculation on Crop Yields

Crops	Fertilizer Supplementation (kg/ha) N	P	K	% Yield Over Control
Wheat	120	-	-	11
	-	-	-	10-30
Rice	120	60	60	23
Maize	-	-	-	34
Sorghum	-	-	-	15-20
Pearlmillet	-	-	-	0-27
Onion	-	50	100	22
Tomato	-	-	-	2-24
Cotton (fibre) irrigated	63	30	-	10-20
Cotton (fibre) Non-irrigated	-	-	-	11-16
Sugarcane	-	-	-	24

Source: Venkataraman and Tilak, 1990.

Shende and Apte (1982) reported yield increase from 6.7 – 71.1 per cent (Table 2). Although phenomenal increase was rewarded but there was also failures at some locations. Those failures were due to single factor that one culture was utilised for various crops and it was assumed that it should serve the purpose of every crop at different parts of the country.

Table 2
Effect of Seed Inoculation with Selected Strains of Azotobacter chroococcum on Different Crops Growth without Fertilizers

Crop/Yield	Location of Field	Control/No Nitrogen	Azotobacter Alone	C.D. at 5%	% Increase in Yield
Sorghum (q/ha)	Pali	12.8	14.0	1.22	9.3
	Dharwar	23.6	32.6	10.56	38.1
Maize (q/ha)	IARI	7.8	13.4	4.80	71.7
	Dharwar	32.0	43.7	9.90	36.5
Cotton (kg/ha)	Surat	1254	1339	241	6.7
	Indore	366	401	104	9.5
	Khandwa	559	708	165	26.6

Source: Shende and Apte, 1982.

Inoculation with *Azotobacter* was found to increase Vitamin C content in tomatoes (Aiyer *et al.,* 1964).

Method of Application

A slurry of carrier based culture is made with minimum amount of water and the seeds are inoculated by mixing with slurry. The seeds are dried in the shade and then sown. For transplanted crops, seedlings are dipped in the slurry for 20-30 minutes and planted immediately. For sugarcane, many packets of culture are recommended at regular intervals in the early stages of growth, second and subsequent inoculation are made by pouring slurry near root zone. The inoculant is also mixed in FYM and broadcasted for the root zone.

Azospirillum **Inoculant**

Azospirillum an associative microphilic nitrogen fixer commonly found in association with the roots of cereals and grasses. High N_2-fixation capacity, low energy requirement and abundant establishment in the roots of cereals and tolerance to high soil temperature (30-40^{0}C) are responsible for its suitability under tropical conditions.

Beneficial Effects

Azospirillum has ability to fix atmospheric-N which remains unaffected by the presence of combined N sources and may account for beneficial response of *Azospirillum* inoculation under saline conditions is possible because strains adapted to these stress condition maintained high nitrogenase activity. The bacterium produces plant growth hormones in pure culture (Tien *et al.,* 1979).

Crop Response

The *Azospirillum* inoculation has been found beneficial in a variety of crops including cereals, forage and other crops. The crop response varies greatly with types of crop and variety, location, season, soil fertility level, native micro-organism interaction, etc. Crop response to *Azospirillum* inoculation is attributed to its ability to fix atmospheric - N and to produce phytohormones.

A number of field experiments conducted on various crops to find out crop response to *Azospirillum* inoculation observed a wide variation in increase in yield (0-64%) over control (Table 3).

Table 3
Effect of Azospirillum Inoculation on Crop Yields

Crops	*N-Fertilizers (kg/ha) Supplementation*	*% Yield Increase Over Control*
Wheat	80	16-20
Rice	40	3-17
Maize	120	14
Barley	40	17
Sorghum	-	23-64
Pearl millet	-	0-37

Source: Venkataraman and Tilak, 1990.

Significant in yield was found at about 50 per cent of the locations. On an average, an increase of about 2-3 q/ha in crop yields and an economy of 20-30 kg N/ha equivalent is possible by *Azospirillum* inoculation. Among various field crops, sorghum and millets respond better than other rainfed conditions. In Tamil Nadu rice responds very well to *Azospirillum* inoculation.

Of all the crops tested, sorghum, pearl millet and finger millet appeared to be consistently responsive to *Azospirillum* at more than one location (Subba Rao *et al.,* 1985; Tilak and Subba Rao, 1987) (Table 4-6).

Table 4
Response of Sorghum var. 'CSH 5' to Inoculation with Azospirillum brasilense on Grain Yield (q/ha)

Treatment	*Udaipur*	*Coimbatore*	*Dharwar*	*Navsari*	*Indore*	*All India Mean*
Uninoculated control (no nitrogen)	26.28	29.43	16.45	16.70	14.67	19.23
A. brassilense	31.85	34.12	20.73	18.33	16.57	22.78
40kg N/ha (urea)	44.80	41.68	30.23	18.63	24.50	30.49
40 kg N/ha + *A. brasilense*	45.78	47.78	31.63	18.63	21.80	31.05
C.D. at 5%	3.25	4.75	4.05	3.50	4.50	-

Table 5

Response of Pearlmillet to Inoculation with Azospirillum brasilense on Grain Yield (q/ha)

Treatment	***Kanpur***	***Parbhani***	***Delhi***	***All India Mean***
Uninoculated control	12.8	14.5	9.8	12.4
A. brasilense	15.5	17.7	11.3	14.3
10 kg N/ha (urea)	16.3	19.5	11.8	15.5
10 kg N/ha + A. Brasilense	19.1	22.8	14.8	17.8
20 kg N/ha (urea)	17.5	22.5	12.5	16.4
20 kg + Azo. Brasilense	18.9	23.2	15.8	18.7
40 kg N/ha (urea)	20.1	24.3	18.5	20.4
C.D. at 5%	2.5	2.9	3.0	2.2

Source: Sirohi; Tilak and Subba Rao, 1987.

It is evident that seen inoculation with *A. Brasilense* increased the grain yield of sorghum and pearlmillet over uninoculated control at all the centres tested. The increase in All India mean grain yield due to seed inoculation over uninoculated control was 17.9 and 15.4, respectively. By the use of this organism as a seed inoculant, savings of 20-30 kg N/ha equivalent can be achieved in these crops.

Seed inoculation in combination with *Azospirillum brasilense* and *Azotobacter chroococcum* produced synergistic effect on yield of maize, sorghum and barley (Tilak *et al.,* 1982).

Method of Inoculation

The most suitable method used for carrier based culture is the seed inoculation. A 10 per cent sugar solution is prepared to serve as sticker for *Azospirillum* on seeds. This solution is sprinkled on the seed required for 1 ha and seeds are spread on a polythene sheet and mixed uniformly. The content of the culture packet are sprinkled over sticker coated seeds and mixed thoroughly. The seeds are dried on gunny bag in shade. After drying, sowing is done immediately.

References

B.C. Biswa, R.K. Tewatia, Naresh Prasad and Soumitra Das, 1994. *Bio-fertilizers in Indian agriculture*. FAI Pub., New Delhi p 43.

K.V.B.R. Tilak and Geeta Singh, 1994. "Bio-fertilizers - research crop and future needs." *Fertlizer News*, 39(4): 11-18.

K.V.B.R. Tilak, 1991. *Bacterial fertilizers*. ICAR Pub., New Delhi p 66.

Chapter 19

Azolla and Blue Green Algae and Rice Cultivation

B.N. Swami

Dept. of Agril. Chem. & Soil Science, RCA, Udaipur

Introduction

Rice is the staple food of more than 60 per cent of world's population with an area of 145 million hectares under its cultivation. In India, it is grown in about 40 million hectares of land with total production of around 60 million tonnes. In Rajasthan it is grown in a very limited area. Increased rice production is essential of mankind is to meet its greatest challenge - feeding an ever-burgeoning world population. Rice is adopted to such a wide range of soil characteristics and grown under such varied soil conditions that atmost all major group of soils are used for its cultivation (Brammer 1978). The rice soil or paddy soil is not a taxonomic name but a generic term like forest soils, grass land soils, etc. (Ghildyal 1982).

Nitrogen is almost universally limit the growth. The demand for measured rice production is being met in many areas by more intensive cropping systems utilising high yielding varieties combined with a greater use of nitrogenous fertilizers. Additors of nitrogen through biological fixation balance the looses of N through harvest and other mechanisms creating a dynamic equilibrium

(Wetsellor 1979). This equilibrium is being disturbed by pressure to increase crop production. The flooded low land rice soil ecosystem is characterised by aerobic and anaerobic zones in three major ecological layers, *viz*. the flooded water and surface of the soil, the anaerobic plough layer and rhizosphere (Venkateraman & Watanabe, 1982). The three biological system that play an active role in rice ecosystem are (a) free living blue green algae, (b) Azolla arabaera symbiosis, (c) hetrotropic bacteria (Subbarao *et al.,* 1993). This deals with the first two.

Blue Green Algae (BGA)

Significance

Blue green algae bio-fertilizer has been proved to be most efficient source of organic nitrogen in low land paddy. The chief agricultural and ecological importance of these algae depends on the ability of certain species to carry out both photosynthesis and nitrogen fixation. Photosynthesis provides the energy required for the nitrogen fixation. The BGA promotes the growth of the paddy crop by supplying fixed nitrogen through exudating about 30 kg N/ha and microbial degradation of dead algae cells. The BGA have also been implicated to benefit the paddy crop by producing growth promoting substances. The BGA inoculation improves the physical conditions of soil and reduces the soil pH, electrical conductivity and exchangeable sodium when applied to saline alkali soils. Extensive field trials conducted in many parts of India on the use of BGA in rice fields indicated that one-third of the recommended nitrogen fertilizer could be conserved without affecting crop productivity through inoculation (Venkataraman 1979). A residual effect of algae has also been observed in subsequent seasons in many locations. Beneficial effect of algae inoculation have also been reported on a number of other crops such barley, oats, tomato, radish sugarcane and maize etc. However, in certain locations, particularly in salt water bodies, they may also aggravate eutrophication problems.

Nature BGA

BGA are either single celled or consist of branched or unbranched filaments. Some of them possess a peculiar structure known as hetrocysts and all heterocystous forms can fix nitrogen from air.

Recently some blue green algae without hetrocysts have also been found to fix nitrogen under special condition take low oxygen tension (anaerobically) or micro aerobically. The algae that are generally used for field applications are species *Authsira, Tolypothrex, Scytonema, Nostoc, Anabaena* and *Pdectnema* as a mixture.

Occurrence

Rice field provides an ideal environment for blue green algae and consequently, abundant in paddy soils than other cultivated soils. Nitrogen fixing BGA are not present in every environment. The grow more abundantly in tropical and sub-tropical regions and that they are less common in temperate and subtemperate regions (Watanobe, 1959). An all India survey of rice fields showed that out of 2,213 soil samples examined, only 33 per cent were found to harbour useful nitrogen fixing blue green algae and their relative abundance showed wide variations.

Cultivation Cycle

Indigenous nitrogen fixing blue green algae show a seasonal periodicity and succession and are often influenced by crop growth and management practices. The maximum algae biomass in rice field has been observed about two weeks or 1 month before transplantation in Japan, between tillering and pamch initiation in single, after pamch initiation in some parts of India. In many areas, N_2 fixing forms have been observed throughout the cultivation cycle, although genetic and specific composition differs and shows a succession.

Environmental Influencing Factors Algae Growth and Establishment

The growth and establishment of algae in a given habitat are greatly influenced by number of physical and chemical factors. Factors most appropriately have been reviewed by Rodger and Kulasooriya (1980). The most important factors known influence the Algae Growth are listed below:

(1) Quality and quantity of light.
(2) Alternate drying and wetting.
(3) Micro-organisms such as protozoa, fungi, bacteria and phages.

(4) Grazers like copepods, ortracods, snails and mosquito larvae.
(5) Chemical factors like soil pH, nutrient status of the soil and redox potential.
(6) Tillage and water management practices.
(7) Type and node of application of inorganic fertilizers of nitrogen phosphorus and potassium.
(8) Pesticides.

Blue Green Algae and Nitrogen Fixation

More than 100 species of blue greens have the ability to fix nitrogen. A nitrogen accretion of 14-50 kg/ha has been attributed to the activities in different localities (Venkataraman, 1982). Blue green algae has ability to produce nitrogenase which is responsible for fixation of nitrogen. The basic pattern or mode of action of nitrogenase appears to be similar irrespective of the source from which it is obtained. Nitrogen fixation and hetrocyst differentiation postulated to be controlled by some regulatory gene, thus having a genetic linkage. During growth, blue green algae liberate large quantities combined nitrogen mainly in the form of polypeptides with less amounts of free animo acids, vitamins and auxin like substances. Approximately 40 per cent of the algal nitrogen has been found to be recovered by the rice crop and addition of ammonium chloride equivalent 100 kg/ha has no adverse effect.

Other Influences of Blue Green Algae

Growth promoting substances are being produced by the blue green algae. Nature of these substances and mode of action is still clear. Soil aggregates has been found improve by the use of blue green algae. A significant reduction in reduced substances like oxidisable matter, sulphides and ferrous iron due to illegal inoculation has also been reported (Aiyear *et al.*, 1972). A wide range of tolerance of blue green algae to a variety of agricultural chemicals has been recorded.

Algae Production Technology and Method of Field Application

Blue green algae are manageable systems and can be produced in bulk with ease where water is available and temperature is suitable.

Depending on the requirements, four methods of algal have been developed *viz.* Trough or tank method, pit method, field method and nursery cum algae method (Subba Rao *et al.*, 1993). The first two methods are essentially for individual farmers and later two are for bulk production on a commercial scale.

Through or Tank Method

This procedure requires following steps:

1. Prepare shallow trays (2m × 3m × 23cm) of galvanised iron sheets or permanent tanks.
2. Place 8-10 kg of soil and mix it well with 200g superphosphate.
3. Add water (5-15cm) to the trays, depending upon the local conditions and rate of evaporation.
4. Correct the pH of the soil if it is acidic and take control measures for parts.
5. After settle down of the soil, sprinkle algae cultural obtained from research laboratory on the surface of standing water and keep the units in the open air completely exposed to sun.
6. Allow to grow algal in a thick mat and period varies with season. During growth period, maintain water level by intermittent watering of require.
7. After the sufficient growth (formation of thick mat), stop water addition and all to in water to evaporate completely in the sun. The dry algae crack in to flakes, which are stored for field use.
8. Fill the trough or try with water and add a small amount of the dried algal flakes as further inoculum. Continue the above process, till soil is exhausted (usually after 3-4 harvests). Replace soil with fresh soil and continue the process as before.

Pit Method

Method is same as in trough method except shallow pits in the ground with thick polythen sheet to hold the water. This method is easy and less expensive to operate by small farmers in their own backyards or farms.

Field Method

The field production of algae is scale up operation of trough or pit method to produce material on large quantities. Adapting this method a record production of 15.6 tonnes/ha of net blue green algae has been obtained by farmers within three months.

Nursery cum Algal Method

Farmers can produce algae and paddy seedlings simultaneously for a 230 m^2 nursery 40 m^2 area by its side cadre bused for algal production which produces 15-20 kg of algal material and sufficient for 1.5 hectares.

Algae are applied at the rate of 10 kg/ha over the standing water in the field one week after transplanting. Sun-dried material can be stored for long and used in the field. The algae material should not be stored in direct contact with chemical fertilizers or other agricultural chemicals.

Azolla

Significance

The recognition of Azolla as an organic manure in rice cultivation was first shown in North Vientnam in 1957. photosynthesis and N-fixation by cultivated Azolla provides for th rice field an important source of organic matter as well as nitrogen and its arbimilation recovers the plant nutrients in the water layer, reducing the loss of fertilizers (LiZhuo, Xin, 1980). However, the N fixing capacity of Azolla varieties with different environmental conductions of rice cellure, the amount of available nitrogen and other nutrients in paddy soils and water layer, the technology of cultivation and utilisation of Azolla and the species of Azolla used for inoculating. Use of Azolla in rice cultivation has been found to benefit in number of ways increased in grain yield of rice, increased in nitrogen efficiency of urea, suppression of weeds etc. Recently, Subbarao *et al.* (1993) reviewed that work of beneficial effect of Azolla in rice cultivation.

What is Azolla?

Azolla is a genus of elegant water ferns that are widely distributed in the tropical and temperate fresh water ecosystems. In fact, it is ominipresent in nature, each leaf has dorsal and ventral lobe. The dorsal lobe is green and has a blue green algal symbient (*Anabaena azollae*) within a central cavity. The heterocyst of the symbiont Anabaena is the site of nitrogen fixation. So far, six extinct species and 25 fossil species of Azolla have been reported (Hill & Gupal, 1967).

Growth Rate and Nitrogen Input

Ashton (1974) reported that at expontial stage the growth rate was 230 mg/g/day and severe cowdung decreased it to 32 mg/g/day. In India, fresh weight of *A. pannata* increase 2-6 fold every week (Singh 1979a). As mentioned earlier, amount of nitrogen fixed found to very widely. Moore (1969) concluded that 100-160 kg N/ha is fixed in 3-4 months when grown in fallow fields. Singh (1979a, b) reported yield of about 30 kg N/ha in 20 days in the planted rice fields.

Factors Affecting the Growth of Azolla

There is a wide variability in the growth of Azolla as it is influenced by number of factors. Singh and Singh (1990) reviewed the research work on factors affecting the growth of Azolla and following factors were recorded to influence the growth of Azolla:

(1) Water
(2) Minerals
(3) Light
(4) Temperature
(5) Salinity
(6) Combined nitrogen

Decomposition of Azolla and Availability of Its N to Rice

The nitrogen in Azolla is available to the rice after decomposition of fern. It decomposes after 8-10 of incorporation into the soil and rice plants and benefited noticeable after 20-30 days. The non-incorporated Azolla also decomposes after mat formation where over cowdung stimulates its decomposition. Singh (1980) reported release of 41-67 per cent of its N within 7-35 days in India. Usually, nitrogen release from fertilizers is faster as compared to Azolla.

Methods of Azolla's Utilisation in Rice Cultivation

Azolla is either grown as green manure in fallow fields and incorporated before transplanting of rice or intercropped along with rice. The later method is also known as cover cropping dual cropping or growing Azolla under rice plants. Application of Azolla before planting is more effective than dual cropping. The dual cropping is more beneficial for medium or long duration varieties then for early duration varieties.

Azolla Green Manuring

Azolla has to be grown initially in small earthen pots near the cultivators field. A simple Azolla nursery method for its large scale multiplication in the field has been evolved by the farmers (Kannaiyan, 1978). The field selected for nursery must be thoroughly prepared and levelled uniformity and divided into one cent plots (20m × 2m) by providing suitable bunds & irrigation channels. Water is maintained at the depth of 10 cm. Ten kilo of fresh cattle dung in 20 litres of water is sprinkled in each plot and Azolla inoculum @ 8 kg is introduced to each plot. Super phosphate (100 g) is applied in three splits at 4 day interval as a top dressing fertilizer for Azolla. Proper insect control measures are used. After 15 days on inoculation it is harvested and introduced into the near field as a source of inoculum. From one harvest, 40-55 kg fresh Azolla is obtained from each plot. Azolla as a green manure should be applied @ 10-12 tonnes/ha. Azolla can be top dressed @ 5-15 tonnes/ha after one month transplanting.

Azolla Dual Cropping

Azolla is the only green manure which can be cultivated as an inter crop with rice in flooded condition and has no deterimental effect on rice, although its biomass is less in planted fields than in unplanted fields (Tilak 1991). The fern is inoculated at the rate 0.5 to 1.0 tonnes/ha one week after transplanting. Super phosphate at 10 kg P_2O_5/ha and furaden 2.5 kg/ha are applied for its rapid growth. Split application of phosphorus produced greater biomass than single application. After formation of a mat in 20-25 days, field is drained off and it is buried into soil manually or with a help of a weeder. However, Azolla mat gets decomposed itself even without incorporation and nitrogen released in water/soil is used by the standing rice crops.

Limitations

Use of Azolla in rice cultivation has many limitations. Tilak (1993) pointed outed following limitations:

(1) Water is prerequisite and as such, it cannot be used for upland rice.

(2) The initial Azolla inoculum requirements of fresh biomass is between 500 and 1000 kg/ha. Therefore, fresh inoculation is to be maintained in nursery plots throughout the year.

(3) Storage of fresh Azolla is also low and hence difficult to transport for long distances.

(4) Temperature higher than 34 $\pm 1^{0}$C in day time is detrimental for its growth.

(5) Its growth is seriously influenced by pest like pyrates and snails and decrease like black rot.

(6) Azolla inoculum consultation production and distribution are highly essential for its utilisation. Consequently, government policy is essential for establishing such net work system at regional or national level.

(7) Lack of efficient Azolla technology which can be easily adopted by the farmers.

(8) Lack of Azolla varieties which can sexually produce spares that can with stand high temperature and phosphorous application.

References

Aiyer, R.S. Saluhudeen, S. and Venkataraman, G.S. 1972. *Indian J. Agri. Sci.* 42: 380.

Ashton, P.J. 1974. In: *The organge river progress report* 123-128.

Brammer, H. 1978. In: *Soils and Rice*, IARI, Los Benos, Lagina, Philippines pp 35-55.

Ghildayal, B.P. 1982. In: Tran. 12th Int. Congr. Soil Science, *Vertisols & rice soils of Tropics* Feb. 8-16, New Delhi.

Hill, L.V. and Gopal, B. 1967. *Can. J. Bol.* 45: 1179.

Kannaiyan, S. 1978. *Bacterial fertilizer*. ECAR, New Delhi p 66.

LiZhuo Xin 1982 In: Transaction 12th Int Congress Soil Science, *Non Symbiotic nitrogen fixation & organic matter in the tropics*, Feb. 8-16, New Delhi.

Moore, A.W. 1969. *Bot Rev*. 35: 17.

Rodger, P.A. and Kulasooriya, S.A. 1980. *Blue green algae and rice*, p 112. IRRI, Los Banos, Philippines.

Singh, P.K. 1979a. In: *Nitrogen & rice* 407-418, IR&I, Las Banos, Philippines.

Singh, P.K. 1979b. In: *Annual review of plant sciences* (ed) C.P. Malik 137-65, Kalyani Publishers, New Delhi.

Singh, P.K. 1980. Proc. Of the Forth Symp. *On Nitrogen Fixation*. Abstract No. 136.

Singh, P.K. and Singh, D.P. 1990. In: *Bio-fertilizers* (Ed. Somani, L.L., Bhandari, S.C. Saxena, S.N. & Vyas, K.K.) Scientific Publisher, Jodhpur.

Subbarao, N.S. Venkataraman, G.S. and Kannaiyan, S. 1993. *Biological nitrogen fixation*, ICAR, New Delhi.

Tilak, K.V.B.R. 1991 *Bacterial fertilizer*, ICAR, New Delhi p 66.

Venakataraman, G.S. 1982. In proceedings of the National symposium on Biological nitrogen fixation pp 17-26, New Delhi.

Venkataraman, G.S. 1979. In *nitrogen and rice*, pp 311-21, IRRI, Los Benos, Los Banos, Philippines.

Venkataraman, G.S. and Watanable, I. 1982. In *Rice research strategies for the future*, pp 317-26, IRRI, Los Banos, Philippines.

Watenabe, A. 1959. *J. Gen. App. Microbiol*. 5:21.

Wetsallar, R. 1979. *Nitrogen cycles in ecosystems: the paddy fields, presented at Scope* UNEP Workshop, Sept. 1979, Stockholm, Sweden.

Chapter 20

Role of PSB and VAM in Improving Phosphate Use Efficiency

L.L. Somani

Dept. of Agril. Chem. & Soil Science, RCA, Udaiupr

Introduction

Phosphorus is the 'master key' element in crop production. It plays a key role in the balanced nutrition of plants. It is reported to be the limiting plant nutrient factor in several soils and is considered to be the key to crop productivity. Application of phosphatic fertilizers is therefore essential for optimum crop yield. The problem of P fertilisation may become serious in coming years because of the fact that manufacture of phosphatic fertilizers requires the use of non-renewable resources such as high grade rock phosphate and sulphur which are getting depleted progressively and becoming costlier. The known reserves and supplies have been estimated to be used up in about 100 years—stranding a population of 20 million. Thereafter, crop yields would be limited by rate at which phosphate is released from insoluble forms in the soil. The situation is further aggravated by the fact that P is readily fixed in the soil and the average utilisation efficiency of added fertilizer P by plants ranges from 15-25 per cent (Kanwar *et al.* 1982).

The importance of micro-organisms in soil nutrient cycling and their role in plant nutrition has been realised for a long time. Their active part in the decomposition and mineralisation of organic matter and release of nutrients is crucial to sustaining the plant productivity upon which we depend for survival. Broadly two groups of micro-organisms are important—(1) those organisms that allow plants to absorb P from sources that are otherwise less available—the phosphate solubilising micro organisms (PSM), and (2) the Vasicular Arbuscular Mycorrhizae (VAM) which assist the plant in absorbing P from regions normally not assesible to plant roots.

Phosphate Solubilising Micro-Organisms (PSM)

Many soil micro-organisms have the capacity to solubilise insoluble inorganic phosphates known to occur in soil. Various bacteria and fungi reported to solubilise different ypes of insoluble phosphates are listed in Table 1. The population of phosphate solubilising micro-organisms is more in the rhizosphere as compared to non-rhizosphere (Swaby and Sperber, 1959). The higher population of phosphate solubilisers in rhizosphere, and release of P there is much benefit to plants because roots can absorb the solubilised P. The soluble P in the non-rhizosphere region, on the other hand, cannot be utilised by plants because of its low mobility.

Table 1

List of Bacteria and Fungi Reported to Solubilise Insoluble Inorganic Phosphates

	Bacteria	**Fungi**
1.	*Achromobacter sp.*	*Aspergillus awamori*
2.	*Aerobacter sp*	*A. carbonum*
3.	*Agrobacterium sp*	*A. flavus*
4.	*Alcaligenes sp.*	*A. fumigatus*
5.	*Bacillus sereus*	*A. niger*
6.	*B. megaterium*	*A. terreus*
7.	*b. mesentricus*	*Candida sp*
8.	*B. polymyxa*	*Cylindrocladium sp*
9.	*B. pulvifacians*	*Fusarium oxysporum*
10.	*B. pumilus*	*Mucor sp*

11.	*B. subtilis*	*Oidiodendrum sp*
12.	*Brevibacterium sp*	*Paecilomyces fusisporus*
13.	*Ewinia sp*	*P. varioti*
14.	*Escherichia sp*	*Papulaspora mytilina*
15.	*E. freundii*	*Penicillum sp*
16.	*E. intermidia*	*P. digitatum*
17.	*Pseudomonas sp*	*Rhizoctonia sp*
18.	*P. liquefaciens*	*Rhizopus sp*
19.	*P. striata*	*Sclerotium rolfsii*
20.	*Serratia phosphaticum*	*Torula thermophils*
21.	*Xanthomonas sp*	

Source: Mishra, 1985.

Mechanism of Phosphate Solubilisation

Different mechanisms have been suggested for the solubilisation of insoluble phosphates by PSM.

Production of Organic Acids

The production of organic acids in the microenvironment around the roots is considered the most important cause of P solubilisation (Mishra, 1985). Organic acids like acetic, lactic, oxalic, succinic, citric etc. produced by PSM possibly lowers pH and help in the formation of stable complexes of such cations as Ca, Mg, Fe and Al (which otherwise fixes P) (Bajpai and Sundara Rao, 1971).

Chelating Effect

It is possible that PSM can produce effective chelating material in the vicinity of rock phosphate of fertilizer material or in the rhizosphere. Under these conditions P could be solubilised and be present in an available form in high enough concentration to be available to plants (Bajpai and Sundara Rao, 1971).

Production of Inorganic Acids

Nitric or sulphuric acid is produced due to oxidation of nitrogenous compounds or of inorganic sulphur by nitrifying bacteria and *thiobacillus* spp respectively. These acids react with insoluble phosphates including rock phosphate and bring about their solubilisation (Somani and Bhandari, 1989).

Hydrogen Sulphide Reaction

Hydrogen sulphide may be formed by reduction of sulphur containing amino acids by several heterotrophic micro-organisms or from sulphate by sulphate reducing bacteria of the genus *Desulfovibrio*. The hydrogen sulphide so produced reduces ferric phosphate to ferrous sulphide with the release of soluble phosphate (Patrick *et al.,* 1973).

Effect of Carbon Dioxide

Soil micro-organisms are known to produce carbon dioxide in the rhizosphere which encourage solubilisation of insoluble phosphates (Stoklasa and Ernest, 1908).

Mineralisation of Organic Phosphorus

Even though it has been shown that some plants have the capacity to utilise certain organic P compounds directly, the bulk of organic phosphorus must be mineralised before it is available to the plants. It has been observed that a reduction in soil organic P content is associated with a simulataneous increase in the number of micro-organisms capable of dephosphorylating these substances (Somani and Sexena, 1971), showing their involvement in the mineralisation process.

Factors Affecting P Solublisation

Energy Source

Phosphate solubilising micro-organisms are heterotrophs. They solubilise insoluble P by secreting organic acids. Hence energy source plays important role in P solubilisation (Ahmed and Jha, 1968).

Nitrogen Sources

Nitrogen is needed by PSM for the synthesis of amino acids, proteins, purine and pyrimidine nitrogenous bases, which they take up in ammonical, nitrate, nitrite or amino form depending upon the enzyme present in their system. Thus P solubilisation is affected depending upon the availability of preferred nitrogen source (Gaur, 1985).

Hydrogen Ion Concentration

Growth and activity of PSM is affected by the pH of the medium. Bacteria prefer neutral or slightly acidic pH but fungi and yeast prefer a pH range of 4-6 (Swaby and Sperber, 1958).

Temperature

The activity of PSM is low at low temperature, which increase with increasing optimum range (20-40^{0}C) beyond which micro-organisms are desiccated (Gaur, 1983, 1985).

Effect of Calcium Carbonate

Presence of calcium carbonate in the medium reduces solubilisation by PSM (Bardiya, 1970).

Kind of Micro-Organisms Involved

Different micro-organisms have been found to differ in their capacity to solublise phosphorus. Many workers found fungi to have more P solubilising capacity than bacteria, actinomycetes or yeast (Wani and Patel, 1979). Arora and Gaur (1979) reported that among the fungi, *Aspergillus awamori* and *Aspergillus niger* were most effective while among bacteria *Pseudomonas striata and Bacillus polymyxa* were the most efficient.

Humic Substances

Presence of humic substances like sodium humate and fulvic acid have been found to improve P solubilisation. Humic substances act as strong complex forming and chelating agent.

Kind of Substrate

The PSM were effective in solubilising tricalcium phosphate, hydroxy apatite, bone meal, iron phosphate and aluminium phosphate (Mehta and Bhide 1970; Gaur *et al.* 1973). Rock phosphate was also solubilised but was found more resistant to be solubilised (Gaur, 1983). The solubilisation of apatites and rock phosphate also depends upon the chemical composition and arrangement of minerals (Singh *et al.,* 1980). Solubilisation of rock phosphate P is also affected by the concentration of P in rock phosphate as well as by the particle size of rock phosphate.

Effect of Pesticides

Studies have revealed that use of diazinon, chloropyriphos, thionacin and trichloronate (1-10 kg/ha) did not affect PSM while lindan improved the population of anaerobic PSM. Simazine and 2-4-D on the other hand reduced the growth of PSM (Gaur, 1990).

Organic Matter

Application of organic matter has been found to improve the physical, chemical and biological properties of soil which will provide a better environment for the growth and activity of the introduced PSM (Gaur, 1990).

Crop Response to PSM

Solublisation from Added Insoluble Sources

Direct application of low grade rock phosphate (which can not be used for manufacture of phosphatic fertilizers) in meeting P deficiency has been found to give response only in acidic soils and not in neutral or alkaline soils. The inoculation of soil with PSM can help in release of P from the added insoluble forms in neutral and alkaline soils. Bardiya (1970) using Mussoorie RP observed significant increase in yield and P uptake by green gram as a consequence of seed inoculation with *Aspergillus awamori* and *Pseudomonas striata*. Sharma and Singh (1971) reported increased yield and P uptake by rice following inoculation with phosphobacterin along with application of bone meal over application of bone meal alone. The PSM also gave good response on the yield of cotton where *Pseudomonas striata* and *Aspergillus awamori* increased the yield of cotton by 71 per cent over control (Kundu and Gaur, 1980).

Solubilisation of Native Insoluble Soil P

The use of PSM to increase the availability of P to crops has been a fairly wide practice in Soviet Union and other East European countries where these micro-organisms are either inoculated to seed or soil. The culture most commonly used is phosphobacterin which consists of spores of *Bacillus megatarium* var. *Phosphaticum.* Mishustin and Naumova (1962) reported significant yield improvement in 30 per cent of the experiments. Sundara Rao and Paul (1959) recorded yield improvements of 7-33 per cent in berseem, maize and wheat using phosphobacterin and Fosfo-24 (a Czechoslovakian culture).

Field Scale Inoculation Technique

Carrier based cultures are mixed with minimum amount of water to form a slurry to facilitate uniform coating of the seeds with the inoculant. The use of 10 per cent sugar/gur in the suspending fluid enhances the survival of PSM on seed. Spread the inoculated seeds on a clean cloth or gunny bag in the shade to facilitate drying avoiding exposure to direct sunlight. The seeds should be sown soon after drying.

In case of transplantation crops such as rice, the roots of the seedlings should be dipped in the culture suspension for 24 hours before transplanting.

The mixing of RP during composting of organic wastes using PSM can result in P-enriched compost comparable to single superphosphate (Mishra *et al.,* 1982). The intense microbial activity during composting is implicated to be involved in the solubilisation.

Response to VAM

The most important feature of VAM is the restricted spread of the fungus within the roots and its extensive penetration in the soil beyond the zone of root exploration. The interconnected network of external hyphae acts as additional attachment and absorbing surface in the soil beyond the depleton zone that otherwise would remain inaccessible to the plant roots. Crush (1974) reported that in phosphorus deficient soil, VAM strongly stimulated nodulation and growth of tropical legumes. The tropical legumes were more dependent on mycorrhizae than temperate ones and this difference was attributed to the fewer root hair development of the tropical species. There appears some special relationship between formation of mycorrhiza and leguminous nodule since only nodulating lines of soybean responded to VAM inoculation (Schenk and Hinson, 1973).

Summary and Conclusion

The problem of phosphorus nutrition of plants is complex because only 15-25 per cent of the added P is utilised by the plants and remaining gets fixed in the soil. There are a variety of micro-organisms in soil which can solubilise insoluble phosphates and make them accessible to plants.

Researches have shown that plants whose roots are infected with VAM are able to take up phosphorus present in very low concentrations in regions beyond the reach of normal roots. The extension of the VAM's ability to form such a symbiotic association to a wide variety of plants would be of great value to agriculture.

Although large amount of data are available on the solubilisation of insoluble phosphates by different micro-organisms, the practice has not got wide spread application. The competitive ability of the inoculated micro-organisms in soil is a major factor. The optimum conditions for the maximum activity of inoculants needs to be established.

References

Ahmed, N. and Jha, K.K. 1968. *J. Gen. Appl. Microbiol*, 14: 89-95.

Arora, D. and Gaur, A.C. 1979. *Indian J. Expt. Biol.* 17: 1258-1261.

Bajpai P.D. and Sundara Rao W.V.B. 1971. *Soil Sci. Plant Nut.*, 17 : 44-45.

Bajpai, P.D. and Sundara Rao, W.V.B. 1971. *Soil Sci. Plant Nut.*, 17: 41-43.

Bardiya, M.C. 1970, Ph.D. Thesis, P.G. School, IARI, New Delhi.

Crush, J.R. 1974. *New Phytol* 73: 743-749.

Gaur, A.C. 1983. *Adv. Soil Sci.* 1: 127-178.

Gaur, A.C. 1985, *Proc. Soil Biol. Symp.* Hissar, pp 125-128.

Gaur, A.C. 1990. *Phosphate solubilising micro-organisms as bio-fertilizer*. Omega Scientific Publishers, New Delhi.

Gaur, A.C.; Madan, M. and Ostwal, K.P. 1973. *Indian J. Expt. Biol.* 11: 427-429.

Kanwar, J.S.,Goswami, N.N. and Kamath, M.B. 1982. *Fert. News*, 27(2): 43-52.

Kundu, B.S. and Gaur, A.C. 1980. *Pl. Soil* 57: 223-230.

Mehta, Y.R. and Bhide, V.P. 1970. *Indian J. Expt. Biol.* 8: 228-229.

Mishra, M.M. 1985. *Proc. Soil Biol. Symp.*, Hissar pp 227-240.

Mishra, M.M., Kapoor, K.K. and Yadav, K.S. 1982. *Indian J. Agric.* Sci. 52: 674-678.

Mishustin, E.N. and Naumova, A.N. 1962. *Mikrobiologiya* 31: 442-452.

Patrik, W.H., Gotoh, S.J. and Williams, B.G. 1973. *Science* 179: 564-566.

Schenk, N.C. and Hinson, J. 1973. *Agron.* J. 65: 849-850.

Sharma, J.P. and Singh, M. 1971. *Indian J. Agron.* 16: 15-18.

Singh, C.P., Mishra, M.M. and Yadav, K.S. 1980. *Ann. Microbiol.*, 131: 289-296.

Somani, L.L. and Bhandari, S.C., 1989. *Soil Micro-organisms and Crop Growth.* Divya Jyoti Prakashan, Jodhpur.

Somani, L.L. and Saxena, S.N. 1971. *J. Indian Soc. Soil Sci.*, 19A 261.

Stoklasa, J. and Ernest, A. 1908 *Jahrb. Wiss. Boton.* 46: 55-102.

Sunmdara Rao W.V.B. and Paul, N.B. 1959. *Proc. ICAR Sem.* pp 326-332.

Swaby, R.J. and Sperber, J.I. 1958. *Nutrition of legumes*, Academic Press, NY.

Swaby, R.J. and Sperber, J.I. 1959. In *Nutrition of Legumes.* Butterworths, London, pp 289-294.

Wani, P.K. and Patil, L.K. 1979. *Natn. Acad. Sci. Lett.*, 2: 360-362.

Chapter 21

Effect of Agronomical Practices on Efficiency of Bio-Fertilizers

L.L. Dhakar
Directorate of Extension Education, RAU, Udaipur

Various agronomic manipulations influence greatly the activities of N-fixing micro-organisms and phosphate solubilising bacterias. The efficiency of N-fixing micro-organism and P-solubilising organisms is influenced by optimum temperature. Delay in sowing or early sowing at sub-optimal temperature reduces activities of micro-organisms. Organic matter addition also increases efficiency of bio-fertilizers. Among fertilizers phosphorous is the most useful nutrient for improving efficiency of bio-fertilizers. Herbicides have adverse effect on bio-fertilizers population and growth. The soil moisture affects both growth and N-fixation. The activity of nitrogenase is inhibited reversibly by moderate deficit of water but severe stress cause irreversible damage.

Introduction

Intensive cultivation of land without conservation of soil fertility and soil structure would lead ultimately to the springing up of deserts. Therefore, integrated use of all the sources such as chemical fertilizers, organic manures, and bio-fertilizers is needed to check the degradation of soil. As Dr. Swaminathan rightly said "New technologies are knowledge rather than capital intensive," the ecologically desirable technologies must involve the substitution of market purchased inputs with farm grown fertilizers and pesticides. Use of micro-organisms like nitrogen fixers, phosphorus solubilisers and cellulose decomposer have been included in bio-fertilizers. Despite the fact that these micro-organisms are present in natural environment, the need for inoculation of host plants by these micro-organisms have been realised due to one or other reason like absence of specific micro-organism, low population presence in soil or unfavourable ecological conditions. The response of bio-fertilizer depends upon its survival competence and capability of applied strain under field conditions. The efficiency also depends to some extent on the quality of bio-fertilizers, its storage and handling after production and agronomic practices. The commonly used bio-fertilizers in India are *Rhizobium, Azotobacter, Azospirillum, Azolla anabaena*, blue green algae and phosphorus solubilising micro-organisms.

Agronomic Practices Influencing Efficiency of Bio-fertilizers

Time of Sowing

Time of sowing is most important non-monetary input to exploit the yield potential of crops. Among the various environmental factors both temperature and light influence the micro-organisms population and N_2-fixation by micro-organisms. The major group of free living nitrogen fixing bacteria are mesophilic with an optimum at 28-30^{0}C, in general, but at 35-40^{0}C in the tropics. The lowest tolerable temperature for the performance of *Azotobacter* is 16^{0}C while the highest is 40-50^{0}C. The nitrogenase activity in *Azospirillum* is sensitive to temperature below 18^{0}C. The nitrogen fixation by per unit bacteroid (*Rhizobium*) is highest at 20^{0}C.The temperature below 20^{0}C adversely affect the symbiosis in tropical legumes. Mesophilic nitrogen fixing blue green algae usually have a temperature optimum around 32.5 - 35^{0}C, apparently ceasing to develop above 40^{0}C.

The optimum activity of phosphorus solubilising fungi is around 30^{0}C whereas that for *P. Striata* (Bacteria) ranged between 29-30^{0}C.

Higher temperature such as at 35 to 40^{0}C greatly reduced their activity and thus phosphate solubilising by these organisms.

Experiment conducted at Ludhiana showed that efficiency of applied *Rhizobium* was higher in case of timely sowing of lentil and under late sowing conditions, number of nodules/plant and dry weight of nodules were reduced correspondingly. The decrease in number of nodules and their weight under late sowing was possibly due to fall in temperature. At Pantnagar from 22 October to 19 November sowing of gardenpea produced more number of nodules and their dry weight. The poor nodulation in case of early sowing was probably due to high soil temperature.

Table 1

Number and Dry Weight of Nodules/Plant of Lentil and Gardenpea as Influenced by Date of Sowing

Date of Sowing	***Lentil***		***Date of Sowing***	***Garden pea***	
	No. of Nodules (g)	***Dry wt. of Nodules (g)***		***No. of Nodules (g)***	***Dry wt. of Nodules (g)***
20 Oct	12.7	8.7	8 Oct.	7.1	9.1
10 Nov.	13.2	8.8	15 Oct.	7.9	13.8
30 Nov.	9.6	6.5	22 Oct.	8.8	23.4
20 Dec.	6.8	4.1	29 Oct.	9.5	26.3
			5 Nov.	9.6	33.4
			12 Nov.	9.5	22.6
			19 Nov.	9.4	23.6

Application of Fertilizers and Organic Matter

Organic Matter

Organic matter is a natural source of inorganic nutrients and microbial energy. The addition of organic matter promotes soil aggregation, soil aeration, water infiltration and water use efficiency which results in better crop growth and higher crop productivity. Numerous studies indicate that organic matter influences the population of micro-organisms. A high degree of correlation has been observed between *Azotobacter* and humus content of soil. Addition of FYM and organic matter increases *Azotobacter* population and enhances its growth and activity. Organic manures stimulates blue green algae (Table 2) and nitrogen fixation Nostoc is stimulated with green manuring and *Anabaena* with rice straw plus ammonium sulphate. Addition of FYM increases the activities of *Rhizobium* and thus number of nodules/plants and the dry weight of nodules in pulses.

Numerous studies reveal that the activity of phosphate solubilising bacteria increases with addition of organic matter. Organic matter provides energy for large number of heterotrophic soil microflora after decomposition.

Table 2

Effect of Organic Manures and Fertilizers on Yield of Rice (t/ha)

Treatment	***0% NPK***	***50% NPK***	***100% NPK***	***Mean NPK***
No manure	0.9	2.3	3.2	2.1
FYM (10 t/ha)	1.3	2.9	3.7	2.6
BGA (13 kg crust /ha)	1.1	2.9	3.4	2.5
FYM + BGA	1.6	3.2	4.2	3.0
Mean	1.2	2.8	3.6	2.6
CD (P=0.05)	Fert 0.15	Manure 0.11	F×M 0.20	

Source: Mishra and Sharma (1997). *J. Indian Soc. Soil Sci.* 45(1): 84-88.

Nitrogen

Nitrogen (ammonium, nitrate and urea) fertilizers reduce nitrogen fixation. However, low amounts of ammonium sulphate, potassium nitrate do not inhibit nitrogenase activity and nitrogen fixation and stimulated the growth of free-living diazotrophic bacteria. Nitrate also inhibit the nitrogenase activity of *Azospirillum*. Several workers reported that large amounts of N fertilizer adversely affects the symbiotic nitrogen fixation in legumes. The presence of excessive nitrogen hampers the nitrogen fixation by blue green algae.

Table 3

Interaction Effects of Bacterial Inoculation and N Levels on Seed Yield of Mustard (q/ha)

Bacterial Inoculation	N (kg/ha)					
	1992-93			1993-94		
	0	30	60	0	30	60
Control	8.64	12.87	17.58	7.96	12.18	16.52
Azotobacter	10.74	16.74	17.54	10.37	15.84	16.69
Azospirillum	10.74	16.85	17.75	10.56	15.84	16.57
CD (P=0.05)	1.24			0.93		

Source: Chauhan, D.R. (1996) *Indian J. Agron.* 41(4) : 620-623.

Experiment conducted at Gurgaon reveal that N-fixing bacteria significantly increased seed of mustard at 0 and 30 kg N/ha. However at 60 kg N/ha, the effect was non-significant.

Phosphorus

Phosphorus is the most essential element as it is directly induced in various metabolic activities of plant, formation of ATP, nucleic acids, lipids and also act as enzyme cofactor.

In legumes, as the process of nitrogen fixation, has a very high energy requirement, the nitrogenase activity is dependent on APT for the production of dinitrogen to ammonia. The increasing levels of phosphorus increases the nodules per plant because nodulating bacteria (*Rhizobium*) requires phosphorus for their own growth and development.

Azotobacter does not develop in soils containing less than 10 ppm of soluble phosphorus *Azotobacter* needs at least 20 ppm phosphorus. Phosphorus has been found to stimulate nitrogen fixation by blue green algae. In flooded soils, addition of phosphorus stimulated nitrogenase activity of the blue green algae.

Experiment conducted at Ludhiana showed that combination of *Rhizobium* and 20kg P_2O_5 gave yield of lentil equivalent to 40 kg P_2O_5 without *Rhizobium.* Treatment with *Rhizobium* inoculation with 20 kg P_2O_5/ha showed nitrogenase activity of 27117 n mol/ha/g dry weight of nodules while it was less in case of uninoculated treatment with 20, 40 and 60 kg P_2O_5/ha.

Table 4

Effect of P-levels and Rhizobium Inoculation on the Yield of Lentil and Nitrogenase Activity (n mol/h/g Dry Weight of Intact Root Nodule)

P_2O_5 (kg/ha)	Grain Yield (t/ha)		Nitrogenase Activity	
	Inoculated	Uninoculated	Inoculated	Uninoculated
0	0.76	0.53	20415	14586
20	1.09	0.77	27117	18164
40	1.12	1.02	32497	22285
60	1.13	1.05	34658	36682

SE for comparing uninoculated with inoculated at same P level = 0.023

SE for comparing P level = 0.038

Source: Dhingra *et al.* (1988). *J. Agric. Sci. Camb.* 110: 141-144.

Molybdenum

Being an integral part of nitrogenase enzyme system, molybdenum is an important factor in the ecology of nitrogen fixing bacteria and blue green algae. Several research workers reported that Mo is indispensable element for nodulation, nitrogen fixation by symbiotic and non-symbiotic systems, and general metabolism in plants as Mo is a part of nitrate reduction enzyme. Several workers reported that 2 ppm application of Mo improved nodulation and dry weight of nodules in pulses.

Iron

Iron is required for nitrogenase and ferrodoxin. Iron is an important constituent of leghaemoglobin and cellular enzyme systems in nodules. The requirement of iron is large for a micronutrient in the range of 2-10 ppm and is used in higher amounts at the time of fixing nitrogen than assimilating ammoniacal nitrogen.

Sulphur

Sulphur is a part of proteins (as- SH groups in enzymes), act as a cofactor in oxidation of pyruvic acid, chlorophyll synthesis and also helps in nodule development. Sulphur has a specific effect on N_2-fixation and marginal deficiency may restrict nitrogenase synthesis.

Weed Control

As weed compete for moisture nutrients and light and affects symbiosis (in legumes), dry matter production and grain yield of crops. Traditionally hand hoeing and weeding was the most common practice for controlling weeds. However, due to non-availability and costly labour, chemical control of weeds through the use of herbicides is fast becoming popular in some crops. The following direct effects of herbicides (pesticides) on soil microbiological aspects, which, in turn, influence, plant growth are (1) changes in population of *Azotobacter, Rhizobium,* cellulolytic micro-organisms and phosphate dissolving micro-organisms which determine soil fertility, (2) changes in number of nodules and lateral roots on roots of nodulating legumes and effect on micorrhizal symbiosis in plants, (3) growth of micro-organisms.

Experiment conducted at Junagarh reveal that application of herbicides for control of weeds in groundnut reduced nodules and nodules weight in comparison to hand weeding and interculture operation.

Water Management

Water stress many affect the survival of rhizobia and *Rhizobium* legume association in many legumes. The soil moisture that is adequate for seed germination is also adequate for bacterial movement and nodule(s) formation. For successful infection, reduced water supply can retard nodule development and lead to lower nitrogen fixation.

Moisture supply not only affects the survival, multiplication and movement of rhizobia, but also nodule size and functioning. The translocation of fixed nitrogen from nodules to legumes is dependent upon transpiration rate and the carbon supply to nodules is affected because of the adverse effect not only on photosynthesis but also on translocation of photosynthate through the phloem to the nodules.

Azotobacter has to show heavy demand on soil moisture. Nitrogen fixation by *Azotobacter* has to be highest at 60 per cent water holding capacity. Wetting and drying cycles favoured N-fixation due to the development of a favourable aerobic anaerobic interface in soil.

Table 5

Effect of Cultural and Chemical Weed Control on Nodulation in Groundnut

Treatment	***Nodule Count per Plant at 90 DAS***	***Dry wt. of Nodules (mg)***
HW (30 DAS)	56.5	6.5
HW (30 DAS) + Interculture (30 DAS)	68.7	9.8
HW + Interculture (20 & 40 DAS)	88.3	11.4
Conventional method	96.3	12.6
HW (2), 20 & 40 DAS + Interculture (30, 40 & 60 DAS)	93.8	13.7
Weed free check	102.3	14.8
Unweeded check	35.5	3.4
Fluchloralin @ 0.675 kg/ha	44.6	3.9
Nitrofen @ 1.875 kg/ha	42.6	3.8
Oxidiazon @ 1.0 kg/ha	39.9	3.9
CD (P=0.05)	12.9	2.6

Source: Malavia & Patel (1989). *Indian J. Agron.* 34(2): 205-208.

The optimum soil moisture content for the nitrogen fixing blue-green algae has to be 80-100 per cent of the soil dry weight. Waterlogging has a still greater effect on their proliferation because of lower oxygen levels. Blue green algae can characteristically withstand desiciation as they usually have thick mucilaginous heaths which enables them to absorb moisture very quickly and loose it very slowly.

Azolla usually needs a certain depth of water in the fields, the ideal being when their root tips touch the soil, as a deeper water results in floating and blowing off by winds.

Chapter 22

Causes of Low Efficiency of Bio-Fertilizers

S.C. Bhandari
Dept. of Ag. Chem. & Soil Science, RCA, Udaipur

Introduction

Chemical fertilizers have had a substantial impact on food production in the recent past and are today an indispensable part of modern agriculture. The green revolution of past half century was fueled by technologies heavily dependent on synthetic fertilizers among many other contributors. There are, on the other hand, vast areas of the developing world where N fertilizers are neither available nor affordable. Economical and environmental considerations as well as sustainability of agriculture dictate the need to integrate it with other sources of nutrients and to derive fuller benefits of the system. Although there are many unknowns in the scientific understandings of bio-fertilizers, but there is scope to improve in future (Figure 1). Full utilization of, and maximal benefit from bio-fertilizer system can be realised only through analysis and resolution of major constraints to their optimal performance in the field, and their adoption and use by the farmers and can be grouped under biological, environmental, methodological production level and socio-cultural constraints.

Figure 1

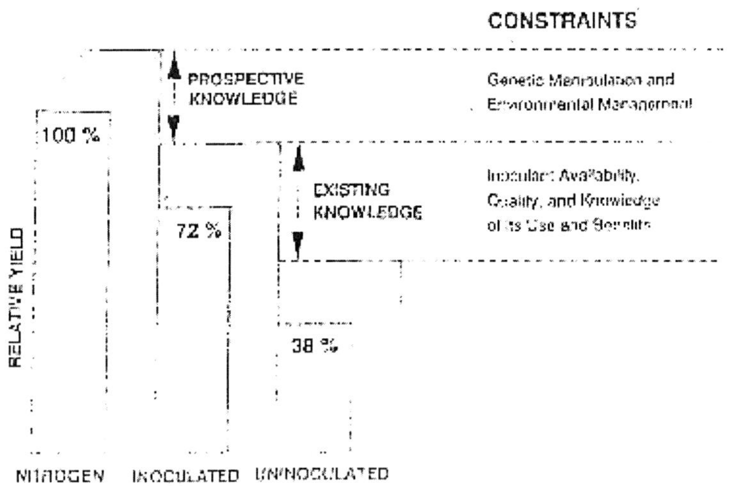

Biological Constraints

Soil is native to BNF micro-organisms and strains existing therein are acclimatised to the soil properties and ecological conditions like temperature, moisture, rainfall pattern etc. Inoculated strains used for treating seeds or field application may be good in potential to contribute toward the BNF and other aspects, but its ability to compete with native population will determine the benefit of inoculation to host crop and also to the succeeding and companion crops. Potentially very good strain may not respond if it can not compete and will be excluded out by native one from the rhizosphere. Therefore, a strain which has wider adaptability with low potential may perform better than strain with high potential and low adaptability.

Compatibility of host plant varieties used in the area differ among the varieties. The compatibility is important as the expression of strain depends on the ability of strains to establish symbiotic association efficiently in case of symbiotic system and ability to interact with micro-organism and root exudates of host plants. Strains which proliferate in the rhizosphere has better chance of contribution failing which genetically potential strain may result in poor response (Gupta *et al.,* 1983). Therefore, it is necessary to evaluate the interaction between variety grown in the area and strain before a strain is released for mass production and distribution to the farmers.

Presence of good population of efficient strain in soil may be another reason of low responce as there is no need of inoculation as the soil is already having efficient strains and under such conditions field response is not expected. Good number of nodules but non-effective ones on account of good population of highly competitive but non-effective native population and less number of effective nodules from effective native and inoculated strains may be another reason for poor response.

Success of use of bio-fertilizer practice depends on the interaction of host and micro-organism. A variety of biological factor may influence the expression of the system. Both partners are subjected to biological constraints such as diseases, insect, nematodes, perdation and growth potential of host etc.

Environmental Constraints

An essential consideration in establishment of BNF system is how they would respond to the adversities of the soil environment to which they are exposed (Dey, 1990). There are large number of factors like nutrition especially N, P, Mo, Fe, S etc. which influence as they are involved in one way or the other.

Deficiency as well as excesses will have effect on the efficiency. Amelioration of limiting factors will result in increased productivity. There are many environmental factors that affect the performance of the inoculants. Major soil factors influencing the efficiency are acidity, alkalinity, salinity, temperature, moisture (Ladha *et al.,* 1992). Organic carbon is another factor which influences the survival and multiplication as most of these organisms are heterotrophs.

Management of soil for raising crops is another factor responsible for low efficiency of system (Sekhon *et al.,* 1990). For successful raising of a crop, various operations are done like tillage, sowing date, weed management, irrigation management, insect management, etc. and have direct or indirect effect on survival, establishment, interaction and expression and thus influence the efficiency of system. Management practices which provided optimum conditions would result in good responses.

Methodological Constraints

Although significant progress has been made in methodology of isolation, identification, maintenance, screening, multiplication, mass production, assessment etc., but still there are many difficulties and obstacles in studying fate of inoculated strains and its assessment under field conditions. Technological standardisation for organisms like *Frankia* is not well established as that of *Rhizobium* and others (Torrey, 1978). Assessment of BNF especially in pasture land and tree legumes is barrier and invent of non-noduating lines will help in assessing potential.

Production Level

The contribution of technologies is governed by its incorporation to farming and depends upon the availability of good cultures to the farmers. Quality cultures are to be regulated by following standards and quality control at each step of production (Motsara *et al.,* 1995). Quality control includes the use of right strain, right type of carrier, free of toxic substances, and contamination with appropriate moisture holding and fineness. Population should be maintained at minimum level upto expiry by proper handling and storage from production to use.

Socio-Cultural Constraints

A successful bio-fertilizer programme must involve, in addition to scientific research, efforts in training, education, outreach and technical assistance. Evaluations of socio-economical constraints are needed to publicise the benefits of technology and provide advance warnings about potential difficulties, facilitating their removal or circumvention.

Conclusion

Integrated nutrient management for sustainable agriculture is essential to reduce dependence on chemical fertilizers and bio-fertilizers being an important component of IPNS, it is necessary to identify the constraints for its proper management.

References

Dey, B.K. 1990. In: *Bio-fertilizers* (Ed. L.L. Somani, S.C. Bhandari, S.N. Saxena and K.K. Vyas) Scientific Publishers, Jodhpur.

Gupta, R.P., Kalra, M.S., Bhandari, S.C. and Khurana, A.S. 1983. *J. Bio. Sci.* 5: 253.

Ladha, J.K., Pareek, R.P. and Beeker, M. 1992. *Adv. Soil Sci.* Academic Press.

Motsara, M.R.; Bhattacharya and Srivastava, B. 1995. *Bio-fertilizer technology marketing and usage - a source book-cum-glossary.* FDCO, New Delhi.

Sekhon, H.S.; Khurana, A.S. and Hill, A. 1990. In: *Bio-fertilizers* (Ed. L.L. Somani, S.C. Bhandari, S.N. Saxena & K.K. Vyas) Scientific Publishers, Jodhpur.

Torrey, J.G. 1978. *Bioscience* 28: 586.

Chapter 23

Evaluation of Efficiency of Bio-Fertilizers

S.C. Bhandari

Dept. of Ag. Chem. & Soil Science, RCA, Udaipur

Introduction

Bio-fertilizers are the products containing living cells of different types of micro-organisms having an ability to mobilise nutritionally important elements from non-usable to usable forms through biological processes. In recent years, bio-fertilizers have emerged as an important component of integrated nutrient supply system and hold promise to improve the crop yields and nutrient supply. There is no difference of opinion about the usefulness of it in Indian agriculture, although the field trials had varied responses. In spite of consistent efforts, the success has not been to the expected level on account of constraints and limitation at various stages, thus failed to harness the full potential of organisms. The evaluation of the technology and its implementation will be necessary to identify the constraints and adoption of suitable measures for improved efficiency (Bergersen, 1980)

Nitrogen

Measurement of Nitrogen Fixation by Direct Means

In case of nitrogen fixing organisms, the fixed nitrogen is utilised by plants and converted into cell constituents and harvestable components. Part of nitrogen fixed remains in soil and may be subjected to variable fate. The efficiency of system can be evaluated by determining total nitrogen, non-protein nitrogen and protein nitrogen based on methods like KJELDAHL method, acid extract, specific enzymatic radiochemical technique, ethanolic extracts etc. Use of heavy isotope and radioactive isotopes N help to quantify the nitrogen fixed and its translocation (Burris and Miller, 1941 and Meeks *et al.,* 1978). The nitrogen analysis of plants, grain, soil and nutrient budgeting including losses help in studying the total contribution and its distribution to the whole system. In this nitrogen is converted into ammonical from and then its quanity is measured by distillation or spectrophomery.

Indirect Measurement of Nitrogen Fixation

The enzyme involved in biological dinitrogen fixation is nitrogenase which consists of Mo-Fe and Fe moiety. This enzyme is non-specific and can reduce other substrates like N_2O, N_3^-, CN^-, NC^-, C_2H_2. Acetylene is reduced to ethylene which can be detected quantitatively at very low concentration using gas liquid chromatograph (Postgate, 1972). It is non-destructive and sample can be assayed repeatedly. It is expressed as nanomoles or micromoles of C_2H_4 per unit of sample (milli litres or milligram of protein of cell or nodule weight) per unit time.

Another indirect method is the measurement of hydrogen, although the relationship between hydrogen, nitrogen and nitrogenase is complex. *In vitro* studies have shown that 25-33 per cent of the electrons used by enzyme are donated to protons, with the consequent production of hydrogen. Hydrogen can be detected using gas chromatography. Other techniques are amperometric, mass spectrometry and tritium exchange (Turner & Gibson, 1980).

Plant Infection for Legumes

Plant infection techniques involves two principles—bacteriological control and environmental conditions like light, temperature, water, carbondioxide, nutrients, pH, combined nitrogen etc. Under a given set of conditions of environment and with no contamination or contamination which does not interfere, the variation in symbiotic parameters like infection, time to initiate nodules, dry weight, nitrogen content, effectiveness of nodulation, acetylene reduction assay and measurement of H_2, O_2 and CO_2 are on account of rhizobia - host plant (Gibson, 1980). There are number of microbiologically controlled systems (Cotton stoppered tubes, Fahraeus slide, plastic pouches, Leonardjar, pots, hydroponics etc.) and non sterile systems (pt culture, soil core, field) which could be adopted for plant infection studies for evaluation of strains.

Enzymes Involved in Metabolism Related to Nitrogenase

Dinitrogen reduction involving nitrogenase can be assayed by assaying the activities of several enzymes involved in the process like ammonia assimilation (*e.g.* Glutamin synthetase and glutamate synthetase), carbon metabolism (*e.g.* PEP carboxylase, invertase) and others (*e.g.* hydrogenase, nitrate reductase, nitrite repluctase).

Leghaemoglobin

Dinitrogen fixation is anaerobic process and leghaemoglobin plays decisive role in regulating the oxygen supply to the bacterioids in nodules. The effectiveness of nodules is correlated by its presence. The assay of it gives idea about the efficiency of root nodule system in fixing nitrogen as nodules deficit in it are ineffective. The leghaemoglohbin can be estimated spectrometry (Bergersen *et al.,* 1973).

Identification of Strains

Strains used as bio-fertilizer contribute to the system only when it can compete and establish with native population of same species and also with other micro-organisms. The degree of contribution correlates with percentage survival and establishment of inoculated strain in competition with native population under existing ecological conditions of moisture, temperature, nutrients, pH, salt concentration, rainfall, agronomic practices, host etc. (Somani, *et al.,* 1990). It involves the identification and quantification of organisms in soil and nodule which can be achieved by the use of serological reactions (asglutination, gelimmunodiffusion, fluorescent antibibody) morphology of culture, production and sensitivity to antibiotics, bacteriocins and bacteriophage, biochemical and mutagenic markers etc. (Schwinghamer and Dudman, 1980). These observations help in determining the extent of establishment of introduced strains under different soil and climatic conditions and help in evaluation of wide spectrum adaptability of strains for recommendation to mass production for supply to farmers for riled applications (Gupta *et al.,* 1983).

Phosphorus

Phosphate Solubilisers

Group of soil micro-organisms improves the fertilizer use efficiency of phosphatic fertilizers either by dissolving as in case of phosphate solubilisers and by help in uptake as in case of mycorrhiza. The solubilisation of soil phosphorus depends on the ability to produce acids both inorganic and organic and by chelating of cation. The efficiecy of inoculum depends on its establishment and multiplication in the rhizosphere which can be enumerated by dilution plat on suitable medium containing phosphorus in insoluble form (Motsara *et al.,* 1995). The efficiency of inoculum can also be evaluated based on the nutrient uptake by crops plants in field/pot trials and soil reservoir after the harvest.

VAM

In case of VAM, the efficiency depends on the degree of establishment of symbiotic relation with roots which can be examined by microscopic examination of stained roots for presence of vesicles and arbuscules (Giovanettic and Mosse, 1980) and also by nutrient uptake by host plants.

Quality Control of Cultures

Evaluation during and after the production of cultures till it is used by the farmer is important for efficiency. Any lapse in the process and during storage and transit may result in contamination, and/or reduction in count resulting in poor response under field trials. BSI, New Delhi has laid out standards for *Rhizobium* and *Azotobacter* cultures which can be met by observing specified quality controls at production level and proper storage till it is used.

Quality controls include assay for bacterial count and presence of contamination, if any. Properly grown and contaminant free broth should be used for mixing with sterile carrier which is free of toxic substances and have been neutralised. Curing is essential to achieve desired population. Storage should be at 25^0C to maintain the desirable population (Bhandari and Somani, 1990). In case of soil based cyanobacteria, the quality can be ensured by periodic microscopic examination of growing cultures in trays, pits or beds and by adopting required insect control measures. Pure cultures from the laboratory should be used whenever the level of other forms of algae exceeds than the desired proportion to ensure good population of specified strains in the product. Storage of culture in dry cool place is essential for the maintenance of quality of cultures.

Economic Yield

It is most important way to evaluate bio-fertilizers form the farmer point of view that he gets better yield compared to other source with maximum benefit cost ratio. With respect to cost of input, bio-fertilizers are least compared to other sources like chemical fertilizers and manures, at the same time application cost is also low. Therefore, if the farmers are getting better returns in term of yield grains or fruits or fodder and also in terms of quality, it should be used.

Conclusion

There are number of ways to evaluate the efficiency of bio-fertilizers to identify the constraints and limitations of low efficiency involving micro-organisms, plant (host) and ecological conditions. None of the individual method can be used to ascertain the efficiency but a combination of two or more methods have to be adopted for the same.

References

Bergersen, F.J., 1980. *Methods for evaluating biological nitrogen fixation*. John Wiley & Sons, New York.

Bergersen., F.J., Turner, G.L. and Appleby, C.A., 1973. *Biochim. Biophys. Acta*. 292: 271.

Bhandari, S.C. and Somani, L.L., 1990. In: *Bio-fertilizers*, Scientific Publisher, Jodhpur.

Burris, R.H. and Miller, C.E., 1941. *Science*, 93: 114.

Gibson, A.H., 1980. In: *Methods for evaluating, biological nitrogen fixation* (F.J. Bergersen, ed), John Wiley & Sons, New York.

Giovanetti, M. and Mosse, B., 1980. *New Phytol*. 84: 489.

Gupta, R.P., Kalra, M.S., Bhandari, S.C. and Khurana, A.S., 1983. *J. Biosci*. J.: 253.

Meeks, J.C., Wolk, C.P. Lockau, W., Schilling, N. Shaffer, P.W. and Wan-Shen, C., 1978. *J. Bacteriol.* 134A 125.

Motsara, M.R., Bhattacharya, P. and Srivastava, P., 1985. *Bio-fertilizer technology, marketing and usage - a source book-cum-Glossary.* Fertilizer Development & Consultation Organisation, New Delhi.

Postage, J.R., 1972. *Methods in enzymology*, Vol. 6B, Academic Press, New York.

Schwinghamer, E.A. and Dudman, W.F., 1980. *Methods for evaluating biological nitrogen fixation* (F.J. Bergerson, ed.), John Wiley & Sons, New York.

Somani, L.L., Bhandari, S.C., Saxena, S.N. and Vyas, K.K., 1990. *Bio-fertilizers*. Scientific Publishers, Jodhpur.

Turnar, G.L. and Gibson, A.H., 1980.

Chapter 24

Production of Microbial Inoculants

U.S. Rawat

Dept. of Ag. Chem. & Soil Science, RCA, Udaipur

Introduction

Biological sources of improving soil fertility for optimum crop production are vital components of integrated plant nutrient system for sustainable agriculture. Other components of IPNS are soil reserves, fertilizers and manures and accretion though precipitation and irrigation water. Among the biological sources, BNF is an economically attractive and ecologically sound system and contributes about 175 million tonnes of N under different systems. Phosphatic inoculants, on the other hand, increase the availability and root accessibility of nutrient. Despite the fact that these micro-organisms are present in the natural soil environment, the need for inoculation of host plant by these micro-organisms have been realised due to one or other reason like absence of specific micro-organism, low population, presence or dominance of inefficient strains, unfavourable ecological conditions (Adkar and Bhardwaj, 1982). The response to microbial inoculants depends on the survival, competitiveness and compatibility of applied strains under agro-ecological conditions of application in addition to their inherent capacity to fix nitrogen or solubilise phosphorus. The efficiency also depends on the quality of the inoculants, their storage and handling after production.

Types of Microbial Inoculants

Microbial inoculants or commonly called bio-fertilizers are biologically active strains of micro-organisms or stores, which may help in increasing crop productivity by way fixation as in case of nitrogen, solubilisation or accessibility as in case of phosphorus, stimulate plant growth or help in decomposition of plant residues. Commercially exploited inoculants are classified as follows.

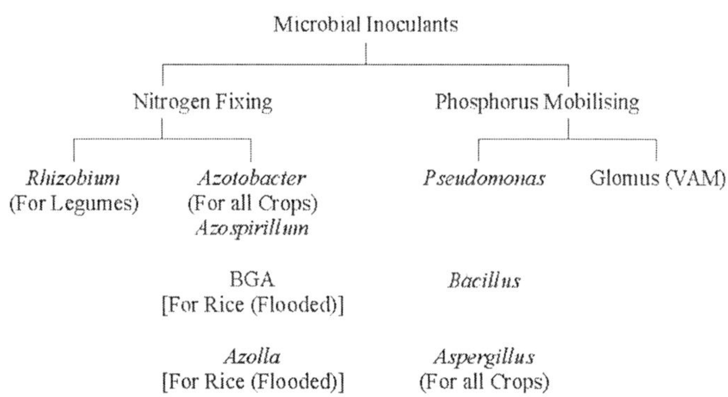

Practical Significance of Microbial Inoculants

Inoculation of legumes with *Rhizobium* as seed treatment at the time of sowing could meet the nitrogen requirement of the host plant upto 80-90 per cent and increases the grain yield by 10-15 per cent (Verma and Bhattacharyya, 1990). Legume crops also benefit to succeeding and companion cereal crops (Patra, 1990) and are used as green manure owing to narrow C:N ratio. Under flooded rice conditions, blue green algae and *Azolla* are important microbial inoculants contributing to the productivity of paddy crop by fixing atmospheric nitrogen, and growth promoting substances (Kaushik, 1990 and Singh and Singh, 1990). Other potent nitrogen fixing organisms are *Azotobacter* and *Azospirillum*. Phosphorus solubilising micro-organisms and VAM fungi have shown positive response with increase in grain yield of various crops.

Requirements of Microbial Inoculants

Although the potential of microbial inoculants was realised long back and earliest documented production of *Rhizobium* dates as early as 1934, commercial production started only in 1956, and standards for carrier based cultures for *Rhizobium* and *Azotobacter* were formulated in late use 1970s only. Although there are number of government and private agencies engaged in production and sale of microbial inoculants (Motsara *et al.,* 1995) the use of these inoculants by users is very limited compared to total acreage under agricultural crops. This gap needs to be narrowed down to reduce dependency on chemical fertilizers, to protect environment from fertilizer pollution and for sustainability of agriculture production. The need for inoculants may also vary with soil properties especially under problematic soils.

Production Technology

The success of microbial inoculants depends on the quality of available inoculants to the farmers at the time of use *i.e.* inoculant packet should have a desired population of specific strain or strains which have been evaluated for their potential and proper use of inoculants by the farmers.

Microbial inoculants should have live cells, hence, they need to be carried from place of manufacture (laboratory) to the field using a suitable carrier. Various methods have been developed to keep the cells alive till inoculants are used such as freeze drying, entrapping cells, pelleting, precoating of seeds, concentrating the cells, organic based carriers etc. Based on the advantages and disadvantages, carrier based inoculants are considered as most suitable for commercial purpose (Thompson, 1980).

Strain Isolation

Strain is the key input for inoculant production. It could be a local strain isolated, identified and evaluated from the soils of the area so that it can survive the competition in a better way when applied or it could be an established strain available from the culture collections of various state universities, national institutes or laboratories (Verma and Bhattacharya, 1992).

Isolation of Strains

(i) *Rhizobium* could be isolated either from the nodules or directly from the soil, however, the isolation from the nodules is the commonly used method using either a defined medium (Brown and Dilworth, 1975) or an undefined medium (Fred *et al.,* 1932). Healthy, pink and unbroken nodules are selected surface sterilised (0.1% Hg C12 or 3-5% H_2O_2), washed repeatedly with sterilised water and dipped in 70 per cent ethanol and washed again. The nodules are then crushed in a small amount of sterile water and plated on the medium (streaked or serial dilution) and incubated at 28^0C. The typical large, white, gummy colonies are picked and purified before they are identified.

The identification methods for rhizobia include microscopic, cultural, serological and plant infection tests (Vincent, 1970). Microscopic observations include staining reaction, morphological features, presence of granules of ß-hydroxy butyrates. Cultural tests include growth on glucose peptone agar, congo red medium, Hofer's alkaline medium, lactore agar medium etc. Serological tests include tube agglutination, fluorescent antibody test, gel immunodiffusion, ELISA etc. The sure way of identification of the rhizobia is to conduct plant infection test under sterilised condition and to see whether isolate produces effective modules on host plant or not. Various methods that could be used are cotton stoppered seedling agar tubes (Thornton, 1930), Fahracus slide technique (Fahraeus, 1957), semi enclosed tubes (Bibson, 1965), plastic pouches (Weaver and Fredrick, 1972), Leonard jar assemblies (Leonard, 1994), pot, tissue culture (Holsten *et al.,* 1971; Philips, 1974a,b; Child and LaRue, 1974), excised root culture technique (Raggio *et al.,* 1975) etc.

(ii) *Azotobacter* spp are isolated from the soil by ten fold serial dilution plating method using a nitrogen free medium (Dalton and Postrate, 1969). The organisms could be isolated by incubating a paste of soil in humid environment prepared in K_2HPO_4 solution and supplemented with starch (Corey, 1959). *Azotobacter* colonies appear as white and turns brown at later stage which is due the production of melanin as the culture grows older.

Organisms are identified based on Microscopic observations like cell size and shape, presence of peritrichous flagella, presence of cyst, poly-ß-hydroxy butyrate, production of gum, serological reactions, growth on nitrogen free medium and biochemical tests.

(iii) *Azospirillum* spp could be isolated from soil or root using enrichment technique on a soil medium with malate as a carbon source. Addition of 0.005 per cent nitrogen to the medium reduces the lag phase. Semi-solid medium (0.05% agar) helps in attaining micro-acrophillic condition required for nitrogen fixation.

(iv) Blue green algae are ubiquitous in nature and can be isolated in pure state by growing in simple inorganic nutrient solution and light. Isolated cultures are purified by repeated plating. Cultures can be identified upto genesic level based on morphological observations.

(v) *Azolla* spp is of common occurrence in ponds, ditches and in rich fields of warm, temperate and tropical regions throughout the world. Species delineating is based primarily upon reproductive structures. The genus is divided into two sections and six living species primarily on the basis of reproductive organs megaspore floats and glochidia (Moore, 1969).

(vi) Phosphate solubilisers - Serial dilutions of soil and rhizosphere soil samples are plated on agar medium containing suspended insoluble phosphate compounds (Pikovskay; medium or Bunt and Rovisa medium). Soil sample is suspended in a known volume of sterile water and dilutions are planted and plates are incubated at $28^0 \pm 2^0$C. The colonies showing halozones are picked, purified and identified following standard procedures of identification.

(vii) VAM spores could be isolated by processing rhizosphere soil and roots of host plants following wet sieving and decantation technique developed by nematologists and was adopted by Gerdemann and Nicolson (1963) for isolating VAM; spores. Other techniques are Doncaster nematode counting dish (Hayman and Stovold, 1979); floatation centrifugation technique with sucrose density gradients (Ohms, 1957); floatation adhesion technique (Sutton and Barron, 1972) etc.

Fungi is identified based on shape of spores, longest dimension of spores at maturity, surface configuration of spores at maturity, number of attached hyphae, from of hyphae near attachment to spore, presence or absence of sporocarps, forms of sporocarps, longest dimension of sporocarps, colour of surface of sporocarps, peridium of sporocarps etc. (Trappe, 1982).

Culture Production and Use

Rhizobium, Azotobacter, Azospirillum and Phosphate Solubilising Bacteria

All the organisms are heterotrophic and can be grown on synthetic media. For commercial production of cultures the utilisation of cheap sources of special nutritive value is found to be more economical.

Any fermentation vessel must be readily sterilised, allow access for inoculation and provide aeration of the cultures. The simplest fermentation vassel is a glass bottle or flask aerated by air bubbles or shaking. Cotton wood plugs can be used provided they are not wetted by the cultures. Use of 1-2 litre glass bottles or flasks is common.

The use of large shakers and glass flasks for commercial production can be defended on the following grounds:

- The quality of broth can easily be varied,
- The volume of the a [illegible] need not be large, and
- The contamina [illegible] ruin whole batch.

However th [illegible] lude:

- The [illegible]
- [illegible]
- The noise of [illegible]
- The risk of contamination increases.
- The labour intensive.

Biologically, the fermentators were reported superior on two important counts (Gulati, 1978):

- The lower proportion of contaminated batches, and
- The superior economy of carbohydrate usage.

Starter culture for fermentor should be suspended in liquid, be in log phase of growth and be sufficiently well grown to provide an inoculum of upto 1 per cent of the total broth to be prepared. Higher inoculum reduce time to maximum growth. Mother culture must be multiplied to a large volume and may be done either on solid or liquid medium and may even involve a multiple stage process if a large inoculum is required.

Apart from amenability of drying and grinding, there are no clear criteria for choice of suitable carriers. Carrier materials for inoculants should meet the following requirements:

- The material should be finely ground to allow through mixing,
- The pH should be readily adjustable to 6.5-7.0,
- A good moisture holding capacity,
- The carrier should be free of toxic materials, and
- The carrier should be sterilisable.

It is necessary to thoroughly test a proposed carrier for suitability. Largely used carriers are peat, lignite, charcoal, organic matter supplemented carriers (Roughley and Vincent, 1967; Kandasamy and Prasad, 1971; Godse *et al.*, 1980; Sharma and Verma, 1979).

Carrier should be dried, preferably air dried or certainly below 100^0C and ground to have desired particle size. Cultures may be prepared either by inoculating a non-sterile carrier or inoculating a sterile carrier. Operations involving the use of a sterilised unpackaged carrier must be considered as an example of unsterillised carrier. Sterilisation methods for packaged carriers usually involve either autoclaving (121^0C) or gamma irradiation (5 Mrad). Inoculants of good quality can be produced with non-sterile carriers as carrier is tored in dired conditions and their natural populations have no opportunity to multiply before culture broth is added. Broth is added, mixed thoroughly, covered to prevent dissipation and held for curing, usually 1 week and packed. Pre-sterilised packets may be inoculated with a needle directly through the wall of the package and point of injection if sterilised and seated using self adhesive label.

Majority of inoculant producers market their product in plastic pouches. A choice of plastic material involves balancing the requirements for gas exchange, moisture retention etc. with strength and resistance to temperature. Various materials available for the purpose are polyethylene polypropylene etc.

Ideally, each separate packet of inoculant should contain the following information:

- Host for which the contents are suitable,
- Quantities of seed to be treated,
- Expire date,
- Instructions for storage and use,
- Certification of a controlling body,
- Batch number,
- Extent of manufacturer's legal responsibility and manufacture's name and address.

For treating seeds, inoculant should be mixed gently with the seeds using minimum quantity of water and suitable adhesive like gum acacia, carboxymethy cellulose, jagger solution etc. taking care to avoid damage to seed coat. Spread the seeds on clean cloth under shade to dry and use immediately for sowing. Inoculum should be applied each year to ensure benefits.

Blue Green Algae

Blue green algae can be produced in bulk with ease where water is available and temperature is suitable (Venkataraman, 1981). Depending on the requirements, 4 methods have been developed (Venkataraman, 1981):

- *Trough or Tank Method*: Prepare shallow trays (2m × 3m ×23cm) of galvanised iron sheet or permanent tanks. Place 8-10 kg of soil (neutral), 200g superphosphate and 5-15 cm of water depending upon evaporation. Insecticide like carbofuran (3% granules) @ 25 g/tray or BHC or malathion or other suitable insecticide is used to control insects. After the soil settle, sprinkle the algae inoculum (mixed culture of *Anabaena, Aulosira* and *Tolypothrix*) or on the surface and keep the troup exposed to sunlight. Maintain the water level till surface is covered with thick mat of algal growth. Allow the water to dry by evaporation and algal flakes are collected and store in bags. Fill the toughs and add a small amount of flakes and inoculum. One harvest gives about 1.5-2 kg of inoculum.

- *Pit Method*: In this method shallow pits layered with polyethylene sheet is used instead of trough. Rest of the procedure is same.
- *Riled Scale Method*: It is scaled up production method of trough method where beds of 40m^2 is used. Rest of the principle is same and one can harvest 16-30 kg/40m^2 flakes during summer months.
- *Nursery-cum-Algal Production*: Algal is grown as mentioned above on a bed (40m^2) parallel to nursery (320m^2). By the time nursery is ready algal inoculum is also ready which will be sufficient for 1.5 hectares.

Algae is to be applied as broadcast over the standing water in the rice field at a rate of 10-15 kg/ha one week after transplanting the seedlings. Addition of excess algae is beneficial and will accelerate the multiplication and establishment. Apply algae for at least three consecutive years.

Azolla

A simple *Azolla* nursery method has been evolved for easy adoption by farmers (Kannaiyan, 1978). The field is thoroughly prepared and levelled uniformaly and then divided into plots (20m × 2m) by providing suitable bunds and irrigation channels. Water is maintained at a depth of 10 cm. Ten kilos of fresh cattle dung mixed in 20 litres of water is sprinkled in each plot and *Azolla* inoculum at 8 kg is introduced to each plot. Superphosphate (100 kg) is applied in three split doses at 4 days interval as a top dressing fertilizer for *Azolla*. For insect control, furadan granules at 100g/plot is applied 7 days after inoculating *Azolla*. After 15 days of inoculation it is harvested and introduced into the main field as a source of primary inoculum. From one harvest, 40-55 kg fresh *Azolla* is obtained from each plot. Four nursery plots are required for raising *Azolla* for inoculation to one hectare main field. Adding cowdung is flooded rice soil system is reported to increase its growth and nitrogenase activity (Kannaiyan, 1978). The use of cowdung and cattle shed water increases its growth during winter (Kannaiyan *et al.*, 1982).

Azolla is grown before transplanting (Basal monocrop) of rice seedlings in fallow fields or as intercrop with rice. Both these practices have been found to be adaptable. The combination of both basal manuring plus intercropping can meet general nitrogen demand of rice crop (Kannaiyan and Subramani, 1987).

Vesicular-Arbuscular Mycorrhiza (VAM)

In root based inoculum production method, a funnel-plant system supports the growth of test seedlings on a sand + soil mixture containing 20-30 spores of a selected VAM fungi held by a piece of glass wool. Root system is checked microscopically for fungal colonisation. Later, the root system together with the adhering soil is manured to form the starter inoculum which is placed at 5 per cent level, 2.5 cm below the soil in big pots supporting the growth of test plants. After 3-4 months the root system to constitute the bulk inoculum. This bulk inoculum may be dispensed for field application in the form of granular preparation, or pelleted with seed and inert material or packaged in polyethylene pouches as semi wet inoculum. Fungus may be multiplied using host plants like maize, clover, cowpea, millets, grasses etc.

BAIF, Pune has developed whose salient features are as:

Mass inocula of *Glomus* and *Gigaspora* may be done on Bahia grass and guinea grass as host plant. The substrate may be soil + perlite (1:1) or soil + Sand (1:3) or vermiculite + peat (4:1). Growth chambers are provided with light intensity at 10-15 K lux: photoperiod of 14 h/day, temperature of 25-28^{0}C, temperature of substrate 28-30^{0}C, pH of substrate 6.5-7.0 and humidity of 70-80 per cent. Microfilters are used for providing bacteria free air. The plants are given fertilizer in the form of urea, rock phosphate/bone meal and muriate of potash and LongAston's nutrient solution for micronutrients. Plants are harvested 75 days after inoculation. Inoculum containing a mixture of VAM fungi hyhpae, spores and VAM infected roots is then dried to 5-10 per cent moisture.

Conclusion

Microbial inoculants contributing through nitrogen fixation and phosphorus mobilisation have been identified as potent organisms to supplement chemical fertilizers or improve fertilizer use efficiency at a very low cost. These inoculants are used as a carrier based using identified better performing strains based on direct and indirect method of assessment.

References

Adkar, S.S. and Bharadwaj, R. 1982. In: *Pulse production: constraints and opportunities* pp 341-49. (Eds.) H.G. Srivastava, S. Bhaskaran, K.K.G. Menon, S. Ramanujam and M.V. Rao. Oxford & IBH Publishing Co. Pvt. Ltd., New Delhi.

Brown, C.M. and Dilworth, M.J. 1975. *J. Gen. Microbiol.* 86: 38-48.

Child, J.J. and LaRue, T.A. 1974. *Pl. Physiol.* 53: 88.

Corey, R.R. 1959. *Microbiology - a laboratory guide.* Gurgess publishing Co., Minnesota, USA.

Dalton, H. and Postagate, J.R. 1969. *J. Gen Microbiol.* 54: 463-473.

Fahraeus, G. 1957. *J. Gen. Microbiol.* 14: 374-81.

Fred, E.B.; Baldwin, I.L. and McCoy, E. 1932. In: *University of Wisconsin studies in science.* No. 6, Madison, Wisconsin, USA.

Gerdemann, J.W. and Nicolson, T.S. 1963. *Trans. Br. Mycol. Soc.* 46: 235-44.

Gibson, A.H. 1965. *Aust. J. Biol. Sci.* 16: 28-42.

Godse, D.R.; More, B.B. and Patil, P.L. 1980. In: *Aspect of biological nitrogen fixation* USA Tech. Series no. 28, Bangalore pp 191-96.

Holsten, R.D.; Burns, R.C.; Hardy, R.W.F. and Hebert, Rr 1971. *Nature* 232: 173-76.

Kandasamy, R. And Prasad, N.N. 1971. *Curr. Sci.* 40: 496.

Kannaiyan, S. 1978. *Farm Science* 5: 19-25.

Kannaiyan, S., and Subramani, S. 1987. ICAR-IARI symposium on National Management in Rice Based Cropping Systems 28-30 Sept., 1987, New Delhi, India.

Kanniayan, S.; Thangarju, M. And Oblisamy, G. 1982. *Nat. Sci. Acad. News letter* 5: 30.

Kaushik, B.D. 1990. In: *Bio-fertilizers* pp 137-54 (Eds.) L.L. Somani, S.C. Bhandari, K.K. Vyas and S.N. Saxena, Scientific Publishers, Jodhpur.

Leonard, L.T. 1944. "Method of testing bacterial cultures and results of test of commercial inoculants," 1943. *USDA Circ. No. 703*, Washington, D.C.

Moore, A.W. 1969. *Bot. Rev.* 35: 17-35.

Motsara, M.R.; Bhattacharyya, P. and Srivastava, B. 1995. *Bio-fertilizer: technology, marketing and usage - a source book-cum-*

glossary. Fertilizer Development and Consultation Organisation, New Delhi, India pp 184.

Ohms, R.E. 1957. *Phytopathology* 47: 751-52.

Patra, D.D. 1990. In: *Bio-fertilizers* pp 113-36 (Eds.) L.L. Somani, S.C. Bhandari, K.K. Vyas and S.N. Saxena, Scientific Publishers, Jodhpur.

Philips, D.A. 1974a. *Pl. Physiol*. 53: 67-72.

Philips, D.A. 1974b. *Pl. Physiol*. 54: 654.

Raggio, M.; Raggio. M. and Tprreu. J.G. 1957. *Aust. J. Bot*. 44: 325-34.

Roughley, R.J. and Vincent, J.M. 1967. *Amer. J. Bot*. 44: 325-34.

Sharma, C.P. and Verma, J. 1979. *Sci. & Cult*. 45: 493-94.

Singh, P.K. and Singh, D.P. 1990. In: *Bio-fertilizers* pp 39-66 (Eds.) L.L. Somani, S.C. Bhandari, K.K. Vyas and S.N. Saxena. Scientific Publishers, Jodhpur.

Suthar, J.C. and Barron, G.L. 1972. *Can. J. Bot*. 50: 1909-1914.

Thompson, J.A. 1980. In: *Methods for evaluating* pp 489-533. *Biological nitrogen fixation* (Ed.). F.J. Bergersen. John Wiley, New York, USA.

Thornton, H.C. 1930. *Ann. Bot*. 44: 385-92.

Trappe, J.M. 1982. *Phytopathology* 72: 1102-08.

Venkataraman, G.S. 1981. *Blue green algae for rice production*. FAO soils Bull. 46: 102.

Verma, L.N. and Bhattacharyya 1992. In: *Fertilizers, organic manures, recyclable wastes and bio-fertilizers* pp 132-147 (Eds.) H.L.S. Tandon, Fertiliser Development and Consultation Organisation, New Delhi, India.

Verma, L.N. and Bhattacharyya, P. 1990. *Fert. News*. 35: 87-97.

Vincent, J.M. 1970. *Mannual for the practical study of nodule bacteria*. IBP Handbook no. 15. Oxford, UK Blackwell.

Weaver, R.W. and Frederick 1972. *P.. Soil* 26: 219.

Chapter 25

Quality Control and Use of Bio-Fertilizers

S.C. Bhandari
Dept. of Agri. Chemistry & Soil Science, RCA, Udaipur

Introduction

The success of bio-fertilizers as supplemental source of nutrients for integrated nutrient supply system under natural farming depends on the presence of desired population of right type of strain in the carrier based culture in active form. The responsibilities of maintaining the standards lies with the producers and government, in addition may regulate it by periodic inspection to safeguard the interests of the farmers. India (Ann; 1977) has set standard of both production and quality testing for selected strains and permits the use of ISI certification mark on achieving the laid standards. Although standards are there, but for the want of proper implementation, the quality of cultures available in market are not to desired standard resulting in poor performance in the field. Thus quality control is important prerequisite for the success of this low cost ecofriendly input under natural farming as a component of IPNS. The controls have to be assured at every stage.

Standards for Quality Testing

In India, bio-fertilizers are manufactured by agricultural universities, agricultural institutions, cooperatives, private companies etc. For the guidelines and to have a minimum standard of quality, the ISI (now BIS) set up an Agricultural Useful Micro-organisms Section Committee which prepared standards for *Rhizobium* and *Azotobacter* in 1977 and were revised in 1986. The abstracts of these standards are given in Table 1.

Table 1

Indian Standard Specifications for Rhizobium and Azotobacter

Parameters	***Rhizobium Inoculant***	***Azotobacter Inoculant***
1. Base	Carrier based	Carrier based
2. Cell number at the time of manufacture	10^8/g carrier within 15 days of manufacture	10^7/g carrier within 15 days of manufacture
3. Cell number at the time of expiry	10^7/g carrier within 15 days before expiry date	10^6/g carrier within 15 days before expiry date.
4. Expiry period	6 months from the date of manufacture	6 months from the date of manufacture.
5. Permissible contamination	No contamination at 10^8 dilution	No contamination at 10^5dilution
6. pH	6-7.5	6.5-7.5
7. Strain	To be identified serologically.	Nothing specific
8. Carrier	Should pass through 150-212 micron.	Should pass through 106 micron.
9. Others	Should give positive test for nodulation and result in 50% or more dry matter than control.	Minimum amount of N_2 fixation not less than 10 mg per gram of sucrose utilised

Source: IS (1868-1978) and IS (1938-1979).

Facilities Required

Quality control is a technical work and needs to have trained personnel and proper laboratory facilities to have effective control. The laboratory should be under the control of government and is to be manned by professional microbiologist along with technical assistants to assist the microbiologist. Laboratory should be equipped with instruments/facilities aseptic cabinet/laminar, antisera facilities, plant growth room facilities for nodulation test, glass-house for experiment, microscope, Kjedahl nitrogen analysis instrument, gas liquid chromatograph, freeze drier, field for field testing etc. (Thompson, 1984). In addition to these routine facilities for a microbiology laboratory are required.

Stages for Quality Control

There are number of stages where organisms are handled or stored and thus may get contaminated or survival is affected. Therefore, it is desirable to assess the quality at all these stages to ensure the detection of contamination or low population. It also helps in identifying the reasons for the low count or contamination and for necessary steps to avoid recurrence of it in subsequent batches. Various stages for control are:

(i) During mother culture stage.
(ii) During carrier selection and standardisation.
(iii) During broth culture stage.
(iv) While mixing of broth with carrier.
(v) During packing.
(vi) During storage.

Tests Required

The quality assurance tests to be performed for *Rhizobium* and *Azotobacter* as per ISI standards are given in Table 2. To have uniformity among batches and among manufacturers, the methods have been outlined for various tests like counting of micro-organisms, serological identification, testing for contamination, nitrogen fixation, carrier quality etc. for quality control in ISI standards and details have been given in sources like Vincent (1970) and Brockwell (1980).

Table 2

Quality Assessment Tests for Rhizobium and Azotobacter

Test	***Observation***	***Expected result***
Rhizobium		
1. Streak onto YEMA	Colony character	Colony should appear as typical rhizobial colony and should not take the colour of congo red.

Test		Observation	Expected result
2.	Gram's staining	Gram's reaction	Gram's negative.
3.	Streak on glucose peptone agar	Growth on medium	Should not grow
4.	pH of carrier	-	6.0-7.5
5.	Total plate count	No. of colonies	10^8/g carrier.
6.	Serological test	-	Agglutinate with nominated antiserum
7.	Nodulation	-	Positive
Azotobacter			
1.	Streak onto Jensen's N-free medium	Colony	*A. Chroococcum* colonies are gummy, raised with or without striations, viscous and often sticky. The pigmentation varies from very light brown to black.
2.	Green's staining	Reaction	Gram's negative.
3.	pH of the carrier	-	6.5-7.5
4.	N-fixation	-	Nitrogen fixed should not be less than 10mg/g sucrose utilised.
5.	Total plate count	-	10^7/g carrier.

Source: IS (1868-1978) and IS (1938-1979).

Strains for Inoculant

The strains to be used for culture production are to be identified ande screened by producer himself. Experiment conducted under AICRP and other projects have identified strains having good performance under field trails at number of locations for a number of years. These strains can be used for manufacture of cultures as well as standards for screening collection of strains for identifying better strains. The identified strains are to be maintained as axenic cultures at low temperature or through lyophilisation. Minimum sub-culturing is desired for degeneration of efficiency.

Regulation of Quality Controls

BIS has prepared specification for bio-fertilizers but no regulatory act like Fertilizer Control Act has been formulated so for. BIS. Does not have network to test the samples and are dependent on universities and institution but the process is not very clear. If any manufacturer gets ISI mark, he continues to use it without routine checking. To rectify this limitation, Ministry of Agriculture, Government of India has established the National Bio-fertilizer Development Centre at Ghaziabad with six regional centres at Bangalore, Bhubaneswar, Jabalpur, Hisar, Imphal and Nagpur. These centres have started quality testing although needs improvement in terms of infrastructural set up and technical quality.

Quality Control for Cultures Other than *Rhizobium* and *Azotobacter*

Commercially exploited bio-fertilizers are *Rhizobium, Axotobacter, Azospirillum*, PSB, VAM, *Azolla* and BGA but standards are available only for first two. *Azolla* and BGA are soil based cultures prepared in open trays or beds or pits exposed to sunlight, while *Azospirillum* and PSB are carrier based as *Rhizobium*. VAM are multiplied on suitable host plant using sterilised soil. In case of BGA, culture is multistrain and quality is maintained with respect to presence of all the four strains in suitable proportion. Proper insect control is done during growth. Cultures are properly dried and stored in cool dry place. These cultures are generally multiplied from Non-bacterial free cultures and inoculum is replaced by laboratory growth culture for mass production when degree of contamination exceeds which can be checked microscopically. *Azolla* are also multiplied in open beds. Inoculum replacement is not frequent and only whebn it has insect/disease spread. *Azospirillum* and PSB are produced aseptically as *Rhizobium* and are carrier based. All regular checks as for *Rhizobium/ Azotobacter* are done to detect contamination to identify strains, to maintain count and for carrier.

Use of Culture

There are many ways of use of culture but sole objective is to have sufficient number of effective strains in soil/rhizosphere soil or on the standing water so that it can have significant contribution. Various methods which have been tried are seed treatment with carried based cultures, soil application, drilling along seed, application along with FYM, pre-treated seed, seed treatment with broth, immobilised cultures etc. for bacterial cultures (Mostara *et al.,* 1985) and application on standing water after transplanting rice, or as green manure before paddy crop or as dual crop etc. for BGA/Azolla (Kaushik, 1990 and Singh and Singh, 1990).

Conclusion

The bio-fertilizers involve the use of living cells and the success of the cultures depends on the number of surviving cells in active form and its establishment on application. The quality control measures are prerequisite for ensuring the standard of cultures. Regulation of standards are equally important to have desired population till the cultures expired especially in country like India where climates are extreme.

References

Anon. (1977) *Indian standard specification for Rhizobium inoculant*, New Delhi, ISI.

Brockwell, J. (1980) In: *Methods for evaluating biological nitrogen fixation* (ed. F.J. Bergersen) John Wiley, New York, USA.

Kaushik, B.D. (1990) In: *Bio-fertilizers* (Ed. L.L. Somani, S.C. Bhandari, S.n. Saxena and K.K. Vyas) Scientific Publishers, Jodhpur.

Motsara, M.R.; Bhattacharya, P. and Srivastava, P. (1995) *Bio-fertilizer technology-cum-glossary*. FDCO, New Delhi.

Singh, P.K. and Singh, D.P. (1990). In: *Bio-fertilizers* (Ed. L.L. Somani, S.C. Bhandari, S.N. Saxena and K.K. Vyas) Scientific publishers, Jodhpur.

Thompson, J.A. (1984). *Production and quality control of carrier based legume inoculant.* ICRISAT, Hydrabad.

Vincent, J.M. (1970). *Manual for the practical study of root nodule bacteria. IBP Handbook No. 15*. Oxford, UK: Blackwell.

Chapter 26

Microbes Chemical Interaction

P.C. Lodha

Dept. of Plant Pathology, RCA, Udaipur

Seed treatment with chemical seed protectants is a normal agriculture practice used to protect the leguminous crop from seed borne pathogens. However, in case of leguminous crop it is also imperative to inoculate legume seeds with effective *Rhizobium* culture for better biological nitrogen fixation.

But the duel treatment of chemical and seed Protectants and *Rhizobium* inoculant, may some time produce a toxic effect to *Rhizobium* population coated over the seed surface and in the *rhizosphere*. Seed Protectants like organo mercuriales, thiram, in some cases systemic fungicides like Ridomil, Bavistin and Benlate affect adversely to symbiotic nodulation and biological nitrogen fixation process due to uncompatibility.

Number of workers have reported that some seed dressing fungicides are toxic to *Rhizobium* spp. Allington (1945) reported that chemicals containing mercury, copper or zinc were extremely toxic to *Rhizobium* spp. used for soybean seed inoculation. Hofer (1958) also found that mercury alone with toxic to symbiotic process while studying the selective action of fungicides on *Rhizobium* from lucerne plant. Wrobel (1963) also tested the compatibility of some organic mercurials and thiuramic seed dressing fungicides with *Rhizobium* of pea and lupin. He observed that these fungicides delayed nodulation. Narayana, Radhakrishna and Rai (1981) tested fungicides on nodulation of cowpea and observed that dithane M-45 stimulated nodulation, whereas, Benlate, Bavistin and sicarol were toxic to *Rhizobium* inoculation Dalela and Lodha (1976) observed the effect of seed dressing fungicides on nodulation and yield of groundnut crop inoculated with *Rhizobium* strain and revealed that maximum inhibition of nodules and minimum yield was recorded in phenyl mercury acetate treatment. However, a combination of phenyl mercury acetate and captan was not found to exhibit any toxic effect on nodulation. These authors further observed that mancozeb alone did not show inhibition of nodules, on the contrary, it enhanced the nodule formation.

Thus, it seems that behaviour of different fungicides with *Rhizobium* seed inoculation is variable from crop to crop and strain to strain and influence the biological nitrogen fixation process.

Thus, the number of new seed dressing fungicides particularly the systemic one are coming in the market. In this situation it is very essential to test the compatibility of chemical seed Protectants with *Rhizobium* strain before these and dressing fungicides are used for duel seed inoculation.

References

Allington, W.B. 1945. "Results of uniform soybean treatment test." Pl. *Dis Reptr* (Suppl. 159) 219-224.

Dalela, G.G. and Lodha, P.C. 1976. "Effect of seed dressing fungicides on nodulation and yield of ground nut crop inoculated with *Rhizobium* strain." *Phytopath Medit.* 15: 127-128.

Narayana, Y.D., Radhakrishnan, D. and Rai, P.V. 1981. "Effect of certain fungicides on nodulation of cowpea (*Vigna anguiculata* L.)" *Curr. Sci.* 10(3); 47-48.

Wrobel, T. 1963. "Influence of fungicides on symbiosis of *Rhizobium* with pea and lupin." *Acti. Microbiol. Polon.* 12: 203-207.

Chapter 27

Biopesticides and Its Role in Organic Farming

H.C.L. Gupta

Prof. & Head, Dept. of Entomology, RCA, Udaipur

Widespread and indiscriminate usage of persistent and toxic chemical insecticides has resulted in contamination of the different components of the environment with the accompanying problems in addition to the target insects becoming resistant to the insecticides thereby rendering them ineffective against these insects. Thus, there is the need to look for the alternative methods and safe insecticides. Biopesticides is an effective alternative of chemical pesticides. The use of biological material such as botanicals and microbes etc. comes under the category of biopesticide. The use of biopesticides has not made adequate progress due to several limitations both at production and at farmers level. Nevertheless lot of potential exists for the development and adoption of biopesticides, since use of renewable natural resources would play a key role in maintaining the sustainability without ecological hazards.

The bioagents such as parasite and predators may be included in the category of biopesticides as some of them can multiply at large level to cater the need of some of the farmers but hereunder those bioagents which can easily multiply formulated and industrialise and included in the category of biopestcides. Some of the pathogens such as protozon, bacteria, virus and fungi are entomogenous which has high degree of insect specificity and formulated as insecticides are the biopesticides, more specifically the microbial pesticides.

In insects, various plant compounds affect nerve axons and synapses (*e.g.* pyrethrins, nicotine), muscles (*e.g.* ryanodine), respiration (*e.g.* rotenone), hormonal balance (*e.g.* juvenile and moulting hormone analogues and antagonists), reproduction (*e.g.* ß-asarone), and behaviour (*e.g.* attractants, repellents, antifeedants). The plant parts, products and compounds, therefore, the biopesticides widely used these days for managing the different kinds of pests. They are biodegradable and leaving no toxic residues in edible parts. They are used as dust or sprays in soil and over plants.

Neem product have been found effective against more than 200 agricultural pests. Similarly extracts from variety of plants show pesticidal activity.

The results of scientists working in different parts of the country showed that the efficacy of *Pongamia pinnata* seed and leaf extract (5%), *Azadirachta indica* seed and leaf extract (5%), *Parthenium* whole plant extract (5%), *Ricinus* leaf extract (5%) and *Adhatoda vassica* leaf extract (5%) give effective reduction of sorhum midge. The neem, kaner and garlic extracts inhibit the feeding of Bihar hairy caterpillar. Plant products such as neem leaves and kernel extract, tobacco decoction, neem oil, karanj extract, mahua oil, thumba oil and margocide are effective against *Antigastra catalaundis*. The tomato, gram, cotton, etc. can be protected against *Heliothis* infestation if sprayed with need leaf or kernal 10 per cent suspension, onion leaves (10%), thur (10%), lantana leaves (10%) extracts.

Addition of neem kernel, neem cake in soil quite effective against soil inhabiting pests such as termite, nematode etc. In addition, they improve the soil fertility. The mustard cake and other botanical cakes besides inhibiting the pest population improve the soil quality.

Use of manures instead of chemical fertilizer have been known to conserve predacious arthropods such as carabid beetles and earthworms. Soil is also a major reservoir for inoculum of bacterial viral and fungal pathogens. Liming of soils helps conservation of baculoviruses. Raising of humidity through irrigation is favourable for germination of fungal pathogens.

Parasitoids of sugarcane leaf hopper *Pyrilla perpusilla* can be conserved by crop residue management *i.e.* leaving the unburnt trash and spreading it back on the field.

Extensive studies have been made with NPV (Nuclear Polyhedrosis Virus) and BT (*Bacillus thuringiensis*). The NPV sprays @ 250 to 450 LE have been reported quite effective against *Heliothis* infesting different crops. *Bacillus thuringiensis* is one of the most effective and extensively used entomobacterial pathogen for control of almost all lepidopterous pests. It is being formulated under the trade names Thrucide, Dipel, Biotrol, Bactospeins in dust, liquid granules or baits and used as other chemical pesticides.

Dispel is a biopesticide contains active ingradient *Beaveria bassiana* which belongs to the class fungi imperfecti. It can be used as spray @ 2-4 ml/litre of water and is effective against some of the coleopterous, hemipterous and lepidopterous insects.

Difflubenzuron is a chitin synthesis inhibitor which is formulated as dust or W.P Feeding of diflubernzuron to larvae results in disturbances in moulting. The effective dose against leaf feeding larvae on cotton, soybean, vegetable crops, forest plants is ranging from 1.5 to 30 g per 100 litre of water.

The biopesticides in general are quite effective against different kinds of pests. They are ecologically least disruptive and highly safe to man and animals. Parasites, predators and honey bees are not affected and no-phytotoxic symptoms have been reported. The soil fertility using or adding some of biopesticides in soil or mixing with manure has also been inhanced.

Index